THE MAMMARY PLAYS

THE MAMMARY PLAYS
PAULA VOGEL

HOW I LEARNED TO DRIVE

THE MINEOLA TWINS

THEATRE COMMUNICATIONS GROUP

The Mammary Plays is published by Theatre Communications Group, Inc.,
520 Eighth Avenue, 24th Floor, New York, NY 10018-4156.

This publication is made possible in part with public funds from the New
York State Council on the Arts, a State Agency.

TCG books are exclusively distributed to the book trade by Consortium Book
Sales and Distribution, 1045 Westgate Drive, St. Paul, MN 55114.

Vogel, Paula.
[Mineola twins]
The mammary plays : two plays / Paula Vogel.
Contents: The Mineola twins — How I learned to drive.
ISBN-13: 978-1-55936-144-6
ISBN-10: 1-55936-144-1
I. Vogel, Paula. How I learned to drive. II. Title.
PS3572.O294M56   1998
812'.54—dc21   97–40169
CIP

Cover design by Chip Kidd
Text design and composition by Lisa Govan

First Edition, March 1998
Fifth Printing, October 2005

For Phyllis

CONTENTS

How I Learned to Drive

1

The Mineola Twins

93

HOW I LEARNED TO DRIVE

This play is dedicated to Peter Franklin.

This play was made possible by generous support from The National Theatre Artist Residency Program administered by Theatre Communications Group and funded by The Pew Charitable Trusts and the John Simon Guggenheim Foundation. It was written and developed at the Perseverance Theatre, Douglas, Alaska; Molly D. Smith, Artistic Director.

How I Learned to Drive was produced in February 1997 by Vineyard Theatre, New York City (Douglas Aibel, Artistic Director; Jon Nakagawa, Managing Director). The set design was by Narelle Sissons, costume design by Jess Goldstein, lighting design by Mark McCullough and original sound design was by David Van Tieghem. Mark Brokaw directed the following cast:

Li'l Bit	Mary-Louise Parker
Peck	David Morse
Male Greek Chorus	Michael Showalter
Female Greek Chorus	Johanna Day
Teenage Greek Chorus	Kerry O'Malley

In April 1997, the Vineyard Theatre production, in association with Daryl Roth and Roy Gabay, moved to the Century Theatre, in New York City. Male Greek Chorus was played by Christopher Duva.

Li'l Bit A woman who ages forty-something to eleven years old. (See Notes on the New York Production.)

Peck Attractive man in his forties. Despite a few problems, he should be played by an actor one might cast in the role of Atticus in *To Kill a Mockingbird*.

The Greek Chorus If possible, these three members should be able to sing three-part harmony.

> **Male Greek Chorus** Plays Grandfather, Waiter, High School Boys. Thirties–forties. (See Notes on the New York Production.)

> **Female Greek Chorus** Plays Mother, Aunt Mary, High School Girls. Thirty–fifty. (See Notes on the New York Production.)

> **Teenage Greek Chorus** Plays Grandmother, high school girls and the voice of eleven-year-old Li'l Bit. Note on the casting of this actor: I would strongly recommend casting a young woman who is "of legal age," that is, twenty-one to twenty-five years old who can look as close to eleven as possible. The contrast with the other cast members will help. If the actor is too young, the audience may feel uncomfortable. (See Notes on the New York Production.)

PRODUCTION NOTES

I urge directors to use the Greek Chorus in staging as environment and, well, part of the family—with the exception of the Teenage Greek Chorus member who, after the last time she appears onstage, should perhaps disappear.

As For Music: Please have fun. I wrote sections of the play listening to music like Roy Orbison's "Dream Baby" and The Mamas and the Papa's "Dedicated to the One I Love." The vaudeville sections go well to the Tijuana Brass or any music that sounds like a *Laugh-In* soundtrack. Other sixties music is rife with pedophilish (?) reference: the "You're Sixteen" genre hits; The Beach Boys' "Little Surfer Girl"; Gary Puckett and the Union Gap's "This Girl Is a Woman Now"; "Come Back When You Grow Up," etc.

And whenever possible, please feel free to punctuate the action with traffic signs: "No Passing," "Slow Children," "Dangerous Curves," "One Way," and the visual signs for children, deer crossings, hills, school buses, etc. (See Notes on the New York Production.)

This script uses the notion of slides and projections, which were not used in the New York production of the play.

On Titles: Throughout the script there are bold-faced titles. In production these should be spoken in a neutral voice (the type of voice that driver education films employ). In the New York production these titles were assigned to various members of the Greek Chorus and were done live.

NOTES ON THE NEW YORK PRODUCTION

The role of Li'l Bit was originally written as a character who is forty-something. When we cast Mary-Louise Parker in the role of Li'l Bit, we cast the Greek Chorus members with younger actors as the Female Greek and the Male Greek, and cast the Teenage Greek with an older (that is, mid-twenties) actor as well. There is a great deal of flexibility in age. Directors should change the age in the last monologue for Li'l Bit ("And before you know it, I'll be thirty-five....") to reflect the actor's age who is playing Li'l Bit.

As the house lights dim, a Voice announces:

Safety first—You and Driver Education.

Then the sound of a key turning the ignition of a car. Li'l Bit steps into a spotlight on the stage; "well-endowed," she is a softer-looking woman in the present time than she was at seventeen.

LI'L BIT

Sometimes to tell a secret, you first have to teach a lesson. We're going to start our lesson tonight on an early, warm summer evening.

In a parking lot overlooking the Beltsville Agricultural Farms in suburban Maryland.

Less than a mile away, the crumbling concrete of U.S. One wends its way past one-room revival churches, the porno drive-in, and boarded up motels with For Sale signs tumbling down.

Like I said, it's a warm summer evening.

Here on the land the Department of Agriculture owns, the smell of sleeping farm animal is thick on the air. The smells of clover and hay mix in with the smells of the leather dashboard. You can still imagine how Maryland used to be, before the malls took over. This countryside was once dotted with farmhouses—from their porches you could have witnessed the Civil War raging in the front fields.

Oh yes. There's a moon over Maryland tonight, that spills into the car where I sit beside a man old enough to be—did I mention how still the night is? Damp soil and tranquil air. It's the kind of night that makes a middle-aged man with a mortgage feel like a country boy again.

It's 1969. And I am very old, very cynical of the world, and

I know it all. In short, I am seventeen years old, parking off a dark lane with a married man on an early summer night.

(Lights up on two chairs facing front—or a Buick Riviera, if you will. Waiting patiently, with a smile on his face, Peck sits sniffing the night air. Li'l Bit climbs in beside him, seventeen years old and tense. Throughout the following, the two sit facing directly front. They do not touch. Their bodies remain passive. Only their facial expressions emote.)

PECK

Ummm. I love the smell of your hair.

LI'L BIT

Uh-huh.

PECK

Oh, Lord. Ummmm. *(Beat)* A man could die happy like this.

LI'L BIT

Well, *don't*.

PECK

What shampoo is this?

LI'L BIT

Herbal Essence.

PECK

Herbal Essence. I'm gonna buy me some. Herbal Essence. And when I'm all alone in the house, I'm going to get into the bathtub, and uncap the bottle and—

LI'L BIT

—Be good.

PECK

What?

8

LI'L BIT

Stop being . . . bad.

PECK

What did you think I was going to say? What do you think I'm going to do with the shampoo?

LI'L BIT

I don't want to know. I don't want to hear it.

PECK

I'm going to wash my hair. That's all.

LI'L BIT

Oh.

PECK

What did you think I was going to do?

LI'L BIT

Nothing. . . . I don't know. Something . . . nasty.

PECK

With shampoo? Lord, gal—your mind!

LI'L BIT

And whose fault is it?

PECK

Not mine. I've got the mind of a boy scout.

LI'L BIT

Right. A horny boy scout.

PECK

Boy scouts are always horny. What do you think the first Merit Badge is for?

LI'L BIT

There. You're going to be nasty again.

PECK

Oh, no. I'm good. Very good.

LI'L BIT

It's getting late.

PECK

Don't change the subject. I was talking about how good I am. *(Beat)* Are you ever gonna let me show you how good I am?

LI'L BIT

Don't go over the line now.

PECK

I won't. I'm not gonna do anything you don't want me to do.

LI'L BIT

That's right.

PECK

And I've been good all week.

LI'L BIT

You have?

PECK

Yes. All week. Not a single drink.

LI'L BIT

Good boy.

PECK

Do I get a reward? For not drinking?

LI'L BIT

A small one. It's getting late.

PECK

Just let me undo you. I'll do you back up.

LI'L BIT

All right. But be quick about it. *(Peck pantomimes undoing Li'l Bit's brassiere with one hand)* You know, that's amazing. The way you can undo the hooks through my blouse with one hand.

PECK

Years of practice.

LI'L BIT

You would make an incredible brain surgeon with that dexterity.

PECK

I'll bet Clyde—what's the name of the boy taking you to the prom?

LI'L BIT

Claude Souders.

PECK

Claude Souders. I'll bet it takes him two hands, lights on, and you helping him on to get to first base.

LI'L BIT

Maybe.

(Beat.)

PECK

Can I . . . kiss them? Please?

LI'L BIT

I don't know.

PECK

Don't make a grown man beg.

LI'L BIT

Just one kiss.

PECK

I'm going to lift your blouse.

LI'L BIT

It's a little cold.

(Peck laughs gently.)

PECK

That's not why you're shivering. *(They sit, perfectly still, for a long moment of silence. Peck makes gentle, concentric circles with his thumbs in the air in front of him)* How does that feel?

(Li'l Bit closes her eyes, carefully keeps her voice calm:)

LI'L BIT

It's . . . okay.

(Sacred music, organ music or a boy's choir swells beneath the following.)

PECK

I tell you, you can keep all the cathedrals of Europe. Just give me a second with these—these celestial orbs—

(Peck bows his head as if praying. But he is kissing her nipple. Li'l Bit, eyes still closed, rears back her head on the leather Buick car seat.)

LI'L BIT

Uncle Peck—we've got to go. I've got graduation rehearsal at school tomorrow morning. And you should get on home to Aunt Mary—

PECK

—All right, Li'l Bit.

LI'L BIT

—*Don't* call me that no more. *(Calmer)* Any more. I'm a big girl now, Uncle Peck. As you know.

(Li'l Bit pantomimes refastening her bra behind her back.)

PECK

That you are. Going on eighteen. Kittens will turn into cats.
   (Sighs) I live all week long for these few minutes with you—you know that?

LI'L BIT

I'll drive.

(A Voice cuts in with:)

Idling in the Neutral Gear.

(Sound of car revving cuts off the sacred music; Li'l Bit, now an adult, rises out of the car and comes to us.)

LI'L BIT

In most families, relatives get names like "Junior," or "Brother," or "Bubba." In my family, if we call someone "Big Papa," it's not because he's tall. In my family, folks tend to get nicknamed for their genitalia. Uncle Peck, for example. My mama's adage was "the titless wonder," and my cousin Bobby got branded for life as "B.B."
   (In unison with Greek Chorus:)

LI'L BIT	GREEK CHORUS
For blue balls.	For blue balls.

FEMALE GREEK CHORUS

(As Mother) And of course, we were so excited to have a baby girl that when the nurse brought you in and said, "It's a girl! It's a baby girl!" I just had to see for myself. So we whipped your diapers down and parted your chubby little legs—and right between your legs there was—

(Peck has come over during the above and chimes along:)

PECK   **GREEK CHORUS**
Just a little bit.   Just a little bit.

FEMALE GREEK CHORUS
(As Mother) And when you were born, you were so tiny that you fit in Uncle Peck's outstretched hand.

(Peck stretches his hand out.)

PECK
Now that's a fact. I held you, one day old, right in this hand.

(A traffic signal is projected of a bicycle in a circle with a diagonal red slash.)

LI'L BIT
Even with my family background, I was sixteen or so before I realized that pedophilia did not mean people who loved to bicycle. . . .

(A Voice intrudes:)

Driving in First Gear.

LI'L BIT
1969. A typical family dinner.

FEMALE GREEK CHORUS
(As Mother) Look, Grandma. Li'l Bit's getting to be as big in the bust as you are.

LI'L BIT
Mother! Could we please change the subject?

TEENAGE GREEK CHORUS
(As Grandmother) Well, I hope you are buying her some decent bras. I never had a decent bra, growing up in the Depression,

and now my shoulders are just crippled—crippled from the weight hanging on my shoulders—the dents from my bra straps are big enough to put your finger in. —Here, let me show you—

(As Grandmother starts to open her blouse:)

LI'L BIT
Grandma! Please don't undress at the dinner table.

PECK
I thought the entertainment came *after* the dinner.

LI'L BIT
(To the audience) This is how it always starts. My grandfather, Big Papa, will chime in next with—

MALE GREEK CHORUS
(As Grandfather) Yup. If Li'l Bit gets any bigger, we're gonna haveta buy her a wheelbarrow to carry in front of her—

LI'L BIT
—Damn it—

PECK
—How about those Redskins on Sunday, Big Papa?

LI'L BIT
(To the audience) The only sport Big Papa followed was chasing Grandma around the house—

.

MALE GREEK CHORUS
(As Grandfather) —Or we could write to Kate Smith. Ask her for somma her used brassieres she don't want anymore—she could maybe give to Li'l Bit here—

LI'L BIT
—I can't stand it. I can't.

PECK

Now, honey, that's just their way—

FEMALE GREEK CHORUS

(As Mother) I tell you, Grandma, Li'l Bit's at that age. She's so sensitive, you can't say boo—

LI'L BIT

I'd like some privacy, that's all. Okay? Some goddamn privacy—

PECK

—Well, at least she didn't use the savior's name—

LI'L BIT

(To the audience) And Big Papa wouldn't let a dead dog lie. No sirree.

MALE GREEK CHORUS

(As Grandfather) Well, she'd better stop being so sensitive. 'Cause five minutes before Li'l Bit turns the corner, her tits turn first—

LI'L BIT

(Starting to rise from the table) —That's it. That's it.

PECK

Li'l Bit, you can't let him get to you. Then he wins.

LI'L BIT

I hate him. *Hate* him.

PECK

That's fine. But hate him and eat a good dinner at the same time.

(Li'l Bit calms down and sits with perfect dignity.)

LI'L BIT

The gumbo is really good, Grandma.

MALE GREEK CHORUS

(As Grandfather) A'course, Li'l Bit's got a big surprise coming for her when she goes to that fancy college this fall—

PECK

Big Papa—let it go.

MALE GREEK CHORUS

(As Grandfather) What does she need a college degree for? She's got all the credentials she'll need on her chest—

LI'L BIT

—Maybe I want to learn things. Read. Rise above my cracker background—

PECK

—Whoa, now, Li'l Bit—

MALE GREEK CHORUS

(As Grandfather) What kind of things do you want to read?

LI'L BIT

There's a whole semester course, for example, on Shakespeare—

(Greek Chorus, as Grandfather, laughs until he weeps.)

MALE GREEK CHORUS

(As Grandfather) Shakespeare. That's a good one. Shakespeare is really going to help you in life.

PECK

I think it's wonderful. And on scholarship!

MALE GREEK CHORUS

(As Grandfather) How is Shakespeare going to help her lie on her back in the dark?

(Li'l Bit is on her feet.)

LI'L BIT

You're getting old, Big Papa. You are going to die—very very soon. Maybe even *tonight*. And when you get to heaven, God's going to be a beautiful black woman in a long white robe. She's gonna look at your chart and say: Uh-oh. Fornication. Dog-ugly mean with blood relatives. Oh. Uh-oh. Voted for George Wallace. Well, one last chance: If you can name the play, all will be forgiven. And then she'll quote: "The quality of mercy is not strained." Your answer? Oh, too bad—*Merchant of Venice*: Act IV, Scene iii. And then she'll send your ass to fry in hell with all the other crackers. Excuse me, please.

(To the audience) And as I left the house, I would always hear Big Papa say:

MALE GREEK CHORUS

(As Grandfather) Lucy, your daughter's got a mouth on her. Well, no sense in wasting good gumbo. Pass me her plate, Mama.

LI'L BIT

And Aunt Mary would come up to Uncle Peck:

FEMALE GREEK CHORUS

(As Aunt Mary) Peck, go after her, will you? You're the only one she'll listen to when she gets like this.

PECK

She just needs to cool off.

FEMALE GREEK CHORUS

(As Aunt Mary) Please, honey—Grandma's been on her feet cooking all day.

PECK

All right.

LI'L BIT

And as he left the room, Aunt Mary would say:

FEMALE GREEK CHORUS

(As Aunt Mary) Peck's so good with them when they get to be this age.

(Li'l Bit has stormed to another part of the stage, her back turned, weeping with a teenage fury. Peck, cautiously, as if stalking a deer, comes to her. She turns away even more. He waits a bit.)

PECK

I don't suppose you're talking to family. *(No response)* Does it help that I'm in-law?

LI'L BIT

Don't you dare make fun of this.

PECK

I'm not. There's nothing funny about this. *(Beat)* Although I'll bet when Big Papa is about to meet his maker, he'll remember *The Merchant of Venice.*

LI'L BIT

I've got to get away from here.

PECK

You're going away. Soon. Here, take this.

(Peck hands her his folded handkerchief. Li'l Bit uses it, noisily. Hands it back. Without her seeing, he reverently puts it back.)

LI'L BIT

I hate this family.

PECK

Your grandfather's ignorant. And you're right—he's going to die soon. But he's family. Family is . . . family.

LI'L BIT

Grown-ups are always saying that. Family.

PECK

Well, when you get a little older, you'll see what we're saying.

LI'L BIT

Uh-huh. So family is another acquired taste, like French kissing?

PECK

Come again?

LI'L BIT

You know, at first it really grosses you out, but in time you grow to like it?

PECK

Girl, you are . . . a handful.

LI'L BIT

Uncle Peck—you have the keys to your car?

PECK

Where do you want to go?

LI'L BIT

Just up the road.

PECK

I'll come with you.

LI'L BIT

No—please? I just need to . . . to drive for a little bit. Alone.

(Peck tosses her the keys.)

PECK

When can I see you alone again?

LI'L BIT

Tonight.

(Li'l Bit crosses to center stage while the lights dim around her. A Voice directs:)

Shifting Forward from First to Second Gear.

LI'L BIT

There were a lot of rumors about why I got kicked out of that fancy school in 1970. Some say I got caught with a man in my room. Some say as a kid on scholarship I fooled around with a rich man's daughter.

(Li'l Bit smiles innocently at the audience) I'm not talking.

But the real truth was I had a constant companion in my dorm room—who was less than discrete. Canadian V.O. A fifth a day.

1970. A Nixon recession. I slept on the floors of friends who were out of work themselves. Took factory work when I could find it. A string of dead-end day jobs that didn't last very long.

What I did, most nights, was cruise the Beltway and the back roads of Maryland, where there was still country, past the battlefields and farm houses. Racing in a 1965 Mustang—and as long as I had gasoline for my car and whiskey for me, the nights would pass. Fully tanked, I would speed past the churches and the trees on the bend, thinking just one notch of the steering wheel would be all it would take, and yet some . . . reflex took over. My hands on the wheel in the nine and three o'clock position—I never so much as got a ticket. He taught me well.

(A Voice announces:)

You and the Reverse Gear.

LI'L BIT

Back up. 1968. On the Eastern Shore. A celebration dinner.

(Li'l Bit joins Peck at a table in a restaurant.)

PECK

Feeling better, missy?

LI'L BIT

The bathroom's really amazing here, Uncle Peck! They have these little soaps—instead of borax or something—and they're in the shape of shells.

PECK

I'll have to take a trip to the gentleman's room just to see.

LI'L BIT

How did you know about this place?

PECK

This inn is famous on the Eastern Shore—it's been open since the seventeenth century. And I know how you like history . . .

(Li'l Bit is shy and pleased.)

LI'L BIT

It's great.

PECK

And you've just done your first, legal, long-distance drive. You must be hungry.

LI'L BIT

I'm starved.

PECK

I would suggest a dozen oysters to start, and the crab imperial . . . *(Li'l Bit is genuinely agog)* You might be interested to know the town history. When the British sailed up this very river in the dead of night—see outside where I'm pointing?— they were going to bombard the heck out of this town. But the town fathers were ready for them. They crept up all the trees with lanterns so that the British would think they saw the town lights and they aimed their cannons too high. And that's why the inn is still here for business today.

LI'L BIT

That's a great story.

PECK

(Casually) Would you like to start with a cocktail?

LI'L BIT

You're not . . . you're not going to start drinking, are you, Uncle Peck?

PECK

Not me. I told you, as long as you're with me, I'll never drink. I asked you if *you'd* like a cocktail before dinner. It's nice to have a little something with the oysters.

LI'L BIT

But . . . I'm not . . . legal. We could get arrested. Uncle Peck, they'll never believe I'm twenty-one!

PECK

So? Today we celebrate your driver's license—on the first try. This establishment reminds me a lot of places back home.

LI'L BIT

What does that mean?

PECK

In South Carolina, like here on the Eastern Shore, they're . . . *(Searches for the right euphemism)* . . . "European." Not so puritanical. And very understanding if gentlemen wish to escort very attractive young ladies who might want a before-dinner cocktail. If you want one, I'll order one.

LI'L BIT

Well—sure. Just . . . one.

(The Female Greek Chorus appears in a spot.)

FEMALE GREEK CHORUS

(As Mother) A Mother's Guide to Social Drinking:

A lady never gets sloppy—she may, however, get tipsy and a little gay.

Never drink on an empty stomach. Avail yourself of the bread basket and generous portions of butter. *Slather* the butter on your bread.

Sip your drink, slowly, let the beverage linger in your mouth—interspersed with interesting, fascinating conversation. Sip, never . . . slurp or gulp. Your glass should always be three-quarters full when his glass is empty.

Stay away from *ladies'* drinks: drinks like pink ladies, slow gin fizzes, daiquiris, gold cadillacs, Long Island iced teas, margaritas, piña coladas, mai tais, planters punch, white Russians, black Russians, red Russians, melon balls, blue balls, hummingbirds, hemorrhages and hurricanes. In short, avoid anything with sugar, or anything with an umbrella. Get your vitamin C from *fruit*. Don't order anything with Voodoo or Vixen in the title or sexual positions in the name like Dead Man Screw or the Missionary. *(She sort of titters)*

Believe me, they are lethal. . . . I think you were conceived after one of those.

Drink, instead, like a man: straight up or on the rocks, with plenty of water in between.

Oh, yes. And never mix your drinks. Stay with one all night long, like the man you came in with: bourbon, gin, or tequila till dawn, damn the torpedoes, full speed ahead!

(As the Female Greek Chorus retreats, the Male Greek Chorus approaches the table as a Waiter.)

MALE GREEK CHORUS

(As Waiter) I hope you all are having a pleasant evening. Is there something I can bring you, sir, before you order?

(Li'l Bit waits in anxious fear. Carefully, Uncle Peck says with command:)

PECK

I'll have a plain iced tea. The lady would like a drink, I believe.

(The Male Greek Chorus does a double take; there is a moment when Uncle Peck and he are in silent communication.)

MALE GREEK CHORUS

(As Waiter) Very good. What would the . . . lady like?

LI'L BIT

(A bit flushed) Is there . . . is there any sugar in a martini?

PECK

None that I know of.

LI'L BIT

That's what I'd like then—a dry martini. And could we maybe have some bread?

PECK

A drink fit for a woman of the world. —Please bring the lady a dry martini, be generous with the olives, straight up.

(The Male Greek Chorus anticipates a large tip.)

MALE GREEK CHORUS

(As Waiter) Right away. Very good, sir.

(The Male Greek Chorus returns with an empty martini glass which he puts in front of Li'l Bit.)

PECK

Your glass is empty. Another martini, madam?

LI'L BIT

Yes, thank you.
  (Peck signals the Male Greek Chorus, who nods) So why did you leave South Carolina, Uncle Peck?

PECK

I was stationed in D.C. after the war, and decided to stay. Go North, Young Man, someone might have said.

LI'L BIT

What did you do in the service anyway?

PECK

(Suddenly taciturn) I . . . I did just this and that. Nothing heroic or spectacular.

LI'L BIT

But did you see fighting? Or go to Europe?

PECK

I served in the Pacific Theater. It's really nothing interesting to talk about.

LI'L BIT

It is to me. *(The Waiter has brought another empty glass)* Oh, goody. I love the color of the swizzle sticks. What were we talking about?

PECK

Swizzle sticks.

LI'L BIT

Do you ever think of going back?

PECK

To the Marines?

LI'L BIT

No—to South Carolina.

PECK

Well, we do go back. To visit.

LI'L BIT

No, I mean to live.

PECK

Not very likely. I think it's better if my mother doesn't have a daily reminder of her disappointment.

LI'L BIT

Are these floorboards slanted?

PECK

Yes, the floor is very slanted. I think this is the original floor.

LI'L BIT

Oh, good.

(The Female Greek Chorus as Mother enters swaying a little, a little past tipsy.)

FEMALE GREEK CHORUS

(As Mother) Don't leave your drink unattended when you visit the ladies' room. There is such a thing as white slavery; the modus operandi is to spike an unsuspecting young girl's drink with a "mickey" when she's left the room to powder her nose.

But if you feel you have had more than your sufficiency in liquor, do go to the ladies' room—often. Pop your head out of doors for a refreshing breath of the night air. If you must, wet your face and head with tap water. Don't be afraid to dunk your head if necessary. A wet woman is still less conspicuous than a drunk woman.

(The Female Greek Chorus stumbles a little; conspiratorially) When in the course of human events it becomes necessary, go to a corner stall and insert the index and middle finger down the throat almost to the epiglottis. Divulge your stomach contents by such persuasion, and then wait a few moments before rejoining your beau waiting for you at your table.

Oh, no. Don't be shy or embarrassed. In the very best of establishments, there's always one or two debutantes crouched in the corner stalls, their beaded purses tossed willy-nilly, sounding like cats in heat, heaving up the contents of their stomachs.

(The Female Greek Chorus begins to wander off) I wonder what it is they do in the men's rooms . . .

LI'L BIT

So why is your mother disappointed in you, Uncle Peck?

PECK

Every mother in Horry County has Great Expectations.

LI'L BIT

—Could I have another mar-ti-ni, please?

PECK

I think this is your last one.

(Peck signals the Waiter. The Waiter looks at Li'l Bit and shakes his head no. Peck raises his eyebrow, raises his finger to indicate one more, and then rubs his fingers together. It looks like a secret code. The Waiter sighs, shakes his head sadly, and brings over another empty martini glass. He glares at Peck.)

LI'L BIT

The name of the county where you grew up is "Horry?" *(Li'l Bit, plastered, begins to laugh. Then she stops)* I think your mother should be proud of you.

(Peck signals for the check.)

PECK

Well, missy, she wanted me to do—to *be* everything my father was not. She wanted me to amount to something.

LI'L BIT

But you have! You've amounted a lot. . . .

PECK

I'm just a very ordinary man.

(The Waiter has brought the check and waits. Peck draws out a large bill and hands it to the Waiter. Li'l Bit is in the soppy stage.)

LI'L BIT

I'll bet your mother loves you, Uncle Peck.

(Peck freezes a bit. To Male Greek Chorus as Waiter:)

PECK

Thank you. The service was exceptional. Please keep the change.

MALE GREEK CHORUS

(As Waiter, in a tone that could freeze) Thank you, sir. Will you be needing any help?

PECK

I think we can manage, thank you.

(Just then, the Female Greek Chorus as Mother lurches on stage; the Male Greek Chorus as Waiter escorts her off as she delivers:)

FEMALE GREEK CHORUS

(As Mother) Thanks to judicious planning and several trips to the ladies' loo, your mother once out-drank an entire regiment of British officers on a good-will visit to Washington! Every last man of them! Milquetoasts! How'd they ever kick Hitler's cahones, huh? No match for an American lady—I could drink every man in here under the table.

(She delivers one last crucial hint before she is gently "bounced") As a last resort, when going out for an evening on the town, be sure to wear a skin-tight girdle—so tight that only a surgical knife or acetylene torch can get it off you—so that if you do pass out in the arms of your escort, he'll end

up with rubber burns on his fingers before he can steal your
virtue—

(A Voice punctures the interlude with:)

Vehicle Failure.
Even with careful maintenance and preventive opera-
tion of your automobile, it is all too common for us to
experience an unexpected breakdown. If you are dri-
ving at any speed when a breakdown occurs, you must
slow down and guide the automobile to the side of the
road.

*(Peck is slowly propping up Li'l Bit as they work their way to
his car in the parking lot of the inn.)*

PECK

How are you doing, missy?

LI'L BIT

It's so far to the car, Uncle Peck. Like the lanterns in the trees
the British fired on . . .

(Li'l Bit stumbles. Peck swoops her up in his arms.)

PECK

Okay. I think we're going to take a more direct route.
    (Li'l Bit closes her eyes) Dizzy? *(She nods her head)* Don't
look at the ground. Almost there—do you feel sick to your
stomach? *(Li'l Bit nods. They reach the "car." Peck gently
deposits her on the front seat)* Just settle here a little while
until things stop spinning. *(Li'l Bit opens her eyes)*

LI'L BIT

What are we doing?

PECK

We're just going to sit here until your tummy settles down.

LI'L BIT

It's such nice upholst'ry—

PECK

Think you can go for a ride, now?

LI'L BIT

Where are you taking me?

PECK

Home.

LI'L BIT

You're not taking me—upstairs? There's no room at the inn? *(Li'l Bit giggles)*

PECK

Do you want to go upstairs? *(Li'l Bit doesn't answer)* Or home?

LI'L BIT

—This isn't right, Uncle Peck.

PECK

What isn't right?

LI'L BIT

What we're doing. It's wrong. It's very wrong.

PECK

What are we doing? *(Li'l Bit does not answer)* We're just going out to dinner.

LI'L BIT

You know. It's not nice to Aunt Mary.

PECK

You let me be the judge of what's nice and not nice to my wife.

(Beat.)

LI'L BIT

Now you're mad.

PECK

I'm not mad. It's just that I thought you . . . understood me, Li'l Bit. I think you're the only one who does.

LI'L BIT

Someone will get hurt.

PECK

Have I forced you to do anything?

(There is a long pause as Li'l Bit tries to get sober enough to think this through.)

LI'L BIT

. . . I guess not.

PECK

We are just enjoying each other's company. I've told you, nothing is going to happen between us until you want it to. Do you know that?

LI'L BIT

Yes.

PECK

Nothing is going to happen until you want it to. *(A second more, with Peck staring ahead at the river while seated at the wheel of his car. Then, softly:)* Do you want something to happen?

(Peck reaches over and strokes her face, very gently. Li'l Bit softens, reaches for him, and buries her head in his neck. Then she kisses him. Then she moves away, dizzy again.)

LI'L BIT

. . . I don't know.

(Peck smiles; this has been good news for him—it hasn't been a "no.")

PECK

Then I'll wait. I'm a very patient man. I've been waiting for a long time. I don't mind waiting.

LI'L BIT

Someone is going to get hurt.

PECK

No one is going to get hurt. *(Li'l Bit closes her eyes)* Are you feeling sick?

LI'L BIT

Sleepy.

(Carefully, Peck props Li'l Bit up on the seat.)

PECK

Stay here a second.

LI'L BIT

Where're you going?

PECK

I'm getting something from the back seat.

LI'L BIT

(Scared; too loud) What? What are you going to do?

(Peck reappears in the front seat with a lap rug.)

PECK

Shhhh. *(Peck covers Li'l Bit. She calms down)* There. Think you can sleep?

(Li'l Bit nods. She slides over to rest on his shoulder. With a look of happiness, Peck turns the ignition key. Beat. Peck leaves

Li'l Bit sleeping in the car and strolls down to the audience.
Wagner's *Flying Dutchman comes up faintly.*
   A Voice interjects:)

Idling in the Neutral Gear.

TEENAGE GREEK CHORUS
Uncle Peck Teaches Cousin Bobby How to Fish.

PECK
I get back once or twice a year—supposedly to visit Mama
and the family, but the real truth is to fish. I miss this the most
of all. There's a smell in the Low Country—where the swamp
and fresh inlet join the saltwater—a scent of sand and cypress,
that I haven't found anywhere yet.

I don't say this very often up North because it will just play
into the stereotype everyone has, but I will tell you: I didn't wear
shoes in the summertime until I was sixteen. It's unnatural
down here to pen up your feet in leather. Go ahead—take 'em
off. Let yourself breathe—it really will make you feel better.

We're going to aim for some pompano today—and I have
to tell you, they're a very shy, mercurial fish. Takes patience,
and psychology. You have to believe it doesn't matter if you
catch one or not.

Sky's pretty spectacular—there's some beer in the cooler
next to the crab salad I packed, so help yourself if you get hungry. Are you hungry? Thirsty? Holler if you are.

Okay. You don't want to lean over the bridge like that—
pompano feed in shallow water, and you don't want to get too
close—they're frisky and shy little things—wait, check your
line. Yep, something's been munching while we were talking.

Okay, look: We take the sand flea and you take the hook
like this—right through his little sand flea rump. Sand fleas
should always keep their backs to the wall. Okay. Cast it in,
like I showed you. That's great! I can taste that pompano now,
sautéed with some pecans and butter, a little bourbon—now—
let it lie on the bottom—now, reel, jerk, reel, jerk—

Look—look at your line. There's something calling, all right.

Okay, tip the rod up—not too sharp—hook it—all right, now easy, reel and then rest—let it play. And reel—play it out, that's right—really good! I can't believe it! It's a pompano. —Good work! Way to go! You are an official fisherman now. Pompano are hard to catch. We are going to have a delicious little—

What? Well, I don't know how much pain a fish feels—you can't think of that. Oh, no, don't cry, come on now, it's just a fish—the other guys are going to see you. —No, no, you're just real sensitive, and I think that's wonderful at your age— look, do you want me to cut it free? You do?

Okay, hand me those pliers—look—I'm cutting the hook— okay? And we're just going to drop it in—no I'm not mad. It's just for fun, okay? There—it's going to swim back to its lady friend and tell her what a terrible day it had and she's going to stroke him with her fins until he feels better, and then they'll do something alone together that will make them both feel good and sleepy. . . .

(Peck bends down, very earnest) I don't want you to feel ashamed about crying. I'm not going to tell anyone, okay? I can keep secrets. You know, men cry all the time. They just don't tell anybody, and they don't let anybody catch them. There's nothing you could do that would make me feel ashamed of you. Do you know that? Okay. *(Peck straightens up, smiles)*

Do you want to pack up and call it a day? I tell you what— I think I can still remember—there's a really neat tree house where I used to stay for days. I think it's still here—it was the last time I looked. But it's a secret place—you can't tell any-body we've gone there—least of all your mom or your sisters. —This is something special just between you and me. Sound good? We'll climb up there and have a beer and some crab salad—okay, B.B.? Bobby? Robert . . .

(Li'l Bit sits at a kitchen table with the two Female Greek Chorus members.)

LI'L BIT

(To the audience) Three women, three generations, sit at the kitchen table.

On Men, Sex, and Women: Part I:

FEMALE GREEK CHORUS

(As Mother) Men only want one thing.

LI'L BIT

(Wide-eyed) But what? What is it they want?

FEMALE GREEK CHORUS

(As Mother) And once they have it, they lose all interest. So Don't Give It to Them.

TEENAGE GREEK CHORUS

(As Grandmother) I never had the luxury of the rhythm method. Your grandfather is just a big bull. A big bull. Every morning, every evening.

FEMALE GREEK CHORUS

(As Mother, whispers to Li'l Bit) And he used to come home for lunch every day.

LI'L BIT

My god, Grandma!

TEENAGE GREEK CHORUS

(As Grandmother) Your grandfather only cares that I do two things: have the table set and the bed turned down.

FEMALE GREEK CHORUS

(As Mother) And in all that time, Mother, you never have experienced—?

LI'L BIT

(To the audience) —Now my grandmother believed in all the sacraments of the church, to the day she died. She believed in Santa Claus and the Easter Bunny until she was fifteen. But she didn't believe in—

TEENAGE GREEK CHORUS
(As Grandmother)—Orgasm! That's just something you and Mary have made up! I don't believe you.

FEMALE GREEK CHORUS
(As Mother) Mother, it happens to women all the time—

TEENAGE GREEK CHORUS
(As Grandmother) —Oh, now you're going to tell me about the G force!

LI'L BIT
No, Grandma, I think that's astronauts—

FEMALE GREEK CHORUS
(As Mother) Well, Mama, after all, you were a child bride when Big Papa came and got you—you were a married woman and you still believed in Santa Claus.

TEENAGE GREEK CHORUS
(As Grandmother) It was legal, what Daddy and I did! I was fourteen and in those days, fourteen was a grown-up woman—

(Big Papa shuffles in the kitchen for a cookie.)

MALE GREEK CHORUS
(As Grandfather) —Oh, now we're off on Grandma and the Rape of the Sa-bean Women!

TEENAGE GREEK CHORUS
(As Grandmother) Well, you were the one in such a big hurry—

MALE GREEK CHORUS
(As Grandfather to Li'l Bit) —I picked your grandmother out of that herd of sisters just like a lion chooses the gazelle—the plump, slow, flaky gazelle dawdling at the edge of the herd—your sisters were too smart and too fast and too scrawny—

LI'L BIT

(To the audience) —The family story is that when Big Papa came for Grandma, my Aunt Lily was waiting for him with a broom—and she beat him over the head all the way down the stairs as he was carrying out Grandma's hope chest—

MALE GREEK CHORUS

(As Grandfather) —And they were *mean*. 'Specially Lily.

FEMALE GREEK CHORUS

(As Mother) Well, you were robbing the baby of the family!

TEENAGE GREEK CHORUS

(As Grandmother) I still keep a broom handy in the kitchen! And I know how to use it! So get your hand out of the cookie jar and don't you spoil your appetite for dinner—out of the kitchen!

(Male Greek Chorus as Grandfather leaves chuckling with a cookie.)

FEMALE GREEK CHORUS

(As Mother) Just one thing a married woman needs to know how to use—the rolling pin or the broom. I prefer a heavy, cast-iron fry pan—they're great on a man's head, no matter how thick the skull is.

TEENAGE GREEK CHORUS

(As Grandmother) Yes, sir, your father is ruled by only two bosses! Mr. Gut and Mr. Peter! And sometimes, first thing in the morning, Mr. Sphincter Muscle!

FEMALE GREEK CHORUS

(As Mother) It's true. Men are like children. Just like little boys.

TEENAGE GREEK CHORUS

(As Grandmother) Men are bulls! Big bulls!

(The Greek Chorus is getting aroused.)

FEMALE GREEK CHORUS

(As Mother) They'd still be crouched on their haunches over a fire in a cave if we hadn't cleaned them up!

TEENAGE GREEK CHORUS

(As Grandmother, flushed) Coming in smelling of sweat—

FEMALE GREEK CHORUS

(As Mother) —Looking at those naughty pictures like boys in a dime store with a dollar in their pockets!

TEENAGE GREEK CHORUS

(As Grandmother; raucous) No matter to them what they smell like! They've got to have it, right then, on the spot, right there! Nasty!—

FEMALE GREEK CHORUS

(As Mother) —Vulgar!

TEENAGE GREEK CHORUS

(As Grandmother) Primitive!—

FEMALE GREEK CHORUS

(As Mother) —Hot!—

LI'L BIT

And just about then, Big Papa would shuffle in with—

MALE GREEK CHORUS

(As Grandfather) —What are you all cackling about in here?

TEENAGE GREEK CHORUS

(As Grandmother) Stay out of the kitchen! This is just for girls!

(As Grandfather leaves:)

MALE GREEK CHORUS

(As Grandfather) Lucy, you'd better not be filling Mama's head with sex! Every time you and Mary come over and start in about sex, when I ask a simple question like, "What time is dinner going to be ready?," Mama snaps my head off!

TEENAGE GREEK CHORUS

(As Grandmother) Dinner will be ready when I'm good and ready! Stay out of this kitchen!

(Li'l Bit steps out.
  A Voice directs:)

When Making a Left Turn, You Must Downshift While Going Forward.

LI'L BIT

1979. A long bus trip to Upstate New York. I settled in to read, when a young man sat beside me.

MALE GREEK CHORUS

(As Young Man; voice cracking) "What are you reading?"

LI'L BIT

He asked. His voice broke into that miserable equivalent of vocal acne, not quite falsetto and not tenor, either. I glanced a side view. He was appealing in an odd way, huge ears at a defiant angle springing forward at ninety degrees. He must have been shaving, because his face, with a peach sheen, was speckled with nicks and styptic. "I have a class tomorrow," I told him.

MALE GREEK CHORUS

(As Young Man) "You're taking a class?"

LI'L BIT

"I'm teaching a class." He concentrated on lowering his voice.

MALE GREEK CHORUS

(As Young Man) "I'm a senior. Walt Whitman High."

LI'L BIT

The light was fading outside, so perhaps he was—with a very high voice.

I felt his "interest" quicken. Five steps ahead of the hopes in his head, I slowed down, waited, pretended surprise, acted at listening, all the while knowing we would get off the bus, he would just then seem to think to ask me to dinner, he would chivalrously insist on walking me home, he would continue to converse in the street until I would casually invite him up to my room—and—I was only into the second moment of conversation and I could see the whole evening before me.

And dramaturgically speaking, after the faltering and slightly comical "first act," there was the very briefest of intermissions, and an extremely capable and forceful and *sustained* second act. And after the second act climax and a gentle denouement—before the post-play discussion—I lay on my back in the dark and I thought about you, Uncle Peck. Oh. Oh—this is the allure. Being older. Being the first. Being the translator, the teacher, the epicure, the already jaded. This is how the giver gets taken.

(Li'l Bit changes her tone) On Men, Sex, and Women: Part II:

(Li'l Bit steps back into the scene as a fifteen year old, gawky and quiet, as the gazelle at the edge of the herd.)

TEENAGE GREEK CHORUS

(As Grandmother; to Li'l Bit) You're being mighty quiet, missy. Cat Got Your Tongue?

LI'L BIT

I'm just listening. Just thinking.

TEENAGE GREEK CHORUS

(As Grandmother) Oh, yes, Little Miss Radar Ears? Soaking it all in? Little Miss Sponge? Penny for your thoughts?

(Li'l Bit hesitates to ask but she really wants to know.)

LI'L BIT

Does it—when you do it—you know, theoretically when I do it and I haven't done it before—I mean—does it hurt?

FEMALE GREEK CHORUS

(As Mother) Does what hurt, honey?

LI'L BIT

When a . . . when a girl does it for the first time—with a man—does it hurt?

TEENAGE GREEK CHORUS

(As Grandmother; horrified) That's what you're thinking about?

FEMALE GREEK CHORUS

(As Mother; calm) Well, just a little bit. Like a pinch. And there's a little blood.

TEENAGE GREEK CHORUS

(As Grandmother) Don't tell her that! She's too young to be thinking those things!

FEMALE GREEK CHORUS

(As Mother) Well, if she doesn't find out from me, where is she going to find out? In the street?

TEENAGE GREEK CHORUS

(As Grandmother) Tell her it hurts! It's agony! You think you're going to die! Especially if you do it before marriage!

FEMALE GREEK CHORUS

(As Mother) Mama! I'm going to tell her the truth! Unlike you, you left me and Mary completely in the dark with fairy tales and told us to go to the priest! What does an eighty-year-old priest know about love-making with girls!

LI'L BIT

(Getting upset) It's not fair!

FEMALE GREEK CHORUS

(As Mother) Now, see, she's getting upset—you're scaring her.

TEENAGE GREEK CHORUS

(As Grandmother) Good! Let her be good and scared! It hurts! You bleed like a stuck pig! And you lay there and say, "Why, O Lord, have you forsaken me?!"

LI'L BIT

It's not fair! Why does everything have to hurt for girls? Why is there always blood?

FEMALE GREEK CHORUS

(As Mother) It's not a lot of blood—and it feels wonderful after the pain subsides . . .

TEENAGE GREEK CHORUS

(As Grandmother) You're encouraging her to just go out and find out with the first drugstore joe who buys her a milk shake!

FEMALE GREEK CHORUS

(As Mother) Don't be scared. It won't hurt you—if the man you go to bed with really loves you. It's important that he loves you.

TEENAGE GREEK CHORUS

(As Grandmother) —Why don't you just go out and rent a motel room for her, Lucy?

FEMALE GREEK CHORUS

(As Mother) I believe in telling my daughter the truth! We have a very close relationship! I want her to be able to ask me anything—I'm not scaring her with stories about Eve's sin and snakes crawling on their bellies for eternity and women bearing children in mortal pain—

TEENAGE GREEK CHORUS

(As Grandmother) —If she stops and thinks before she takes her knickers off, maybe someone in this family will finish high school!

(Li'l Bit knows what is about to happen and starts to retreat from the scene at this point.)

FEMALE GREEK CHORUS

(As Mother) Mother! If you and Daddy had helped me—I wouldn't have had to marry that—that no-good-son-of-a—

TEENAGE GREEK CHORUS

(As Grandmother) —He was good enough for you on a full moon! I hold you responsible!

FEMALE GREEK CHORUS

(As Mother) —You could have helped me! You could have told me something about the facts of life!

TEENAGE GREEK CHORUS

(As Grandmother) —I told you what my mother told me! A girl with her skirt up can outrun a man with his pants down!

(The Male Greek Chorus enters the fray; L'il Bit edges further downstage.)

FEMALE GREEK CHORUS

(As Mother) And when I turned to you for a little help, all I got afterwards was—

MALE GREEK CHORUS

(As Grandfather) You Made Your Bed; Now Lie On It!

(The Greek Chorus freezes, mouths open, argumentatively.)

LI'L BIT

(To the audience) Oh, please! I still can't bear to listen to it, after all these years—

(The Male Greek Chorus "unfreezes," but out of his open mouth, as if to his surprise, comes a base refrain from a Motown song.)

MALE GREEK CHORUS
"Do-Bee-Do-Wah!"

(The Female Greek Chorus member is also surprised; but she, too, unfreezes.)

FEMALE GREEK CHORUS
"Shoo-doo-be-doo-be-doo; shoo-doo-be-doo-be-doo."

(The Male and Female Greek Chorus members continue with their harmony, until the Teenage member of the Chorus starts in with Motown lyrics such as "Dedicated to the One I Love," or "In the Still of the Night," or "Hold Me"—any Sam Cooke will do. The three modulate down into three part harmony, softly, until they are submerged by the actual recording playing over the radio in the car in which Uncle Peck sits in the driver's seat, waiting. Li'l Bit sits in the passenger's seat.)

LI'L BIT
Ahh. That's better.

(Uncle Peck reaches over and turns the volume down; to Li'l Bit:)

PECK
How can you hear yourself think?

*(Li'l Bit does not answer.
A Voice insinuates itself in the pause:)*

Before You Drive.
Always check under your car for obstructions—broken bottles, fallen tree branches, and the bodies of small children. Each year hundreds of children are crushed beneath the wheels of unwary drivers in their own driveways. Children depend on *you* to watch them.

*(Pause.
The Voice continues:)*

You and the Reverse Gear.

(In the following section, it would be nice to have slides of erotic photographs of women and cars: women posed over the hood; women draped along the sideboards; women with water hoses spraying the car; and the actress playing Li'l Bit with a Bel Air or any 1950s car one can find for the finale.)

LI'L BIT

1967. In a parking lot of the Beltsville Agricultural Farms. The Initiation into a Boy's First Love.

PECK

(With a soft look on his face) Of course, my favorite car will always be the '56 Bel Air Sports Coupe. Chevy sold more '55s, but the '56!—a V-8 with Corvette option, 225 horsepower; went from zero to sixty miles per hour in 8.9 seconds.

LI'L BIT

(To the audience) Long after a mother's tits, but before a woman's breasts:

PECK

Super-Turbo-Fire! What a Power Pack—mechanical lifters, twin four-barrel carbs, lightweight valves, dual exhausts—

LI'L BIT

(To the audience) After the milk but before the beer:

PECK

A specific intake manifold, higher-lift camshaft, and the tightest squeeze Chevy had ever made—

LI'L BIT

(To the audience) Long after he's squeezed down the birth canal but before he's pushed his way back in: The boy falls in love with the thing that bears his weight with speed.

PECK

I want you to know your automobile inside and out. —Are you there? Li'l Bit?

(Slides end here.)

LI'L BIT

—What?

PECK

You're drifting. I need you to concentrate.

LI'L BIT

Sorry.

PECK

Okay. Get into the driver's seat. *(Li'l Bit does)* Okay. Now. Show me what you're going to do before you start the car.

(Li'l Bit sits, with her hands in her lap. She starts to giggle.)

LI'L BIT

I don't know, Uncle Peck.

PECK

Now, come on. What's the first thing you're going to adjust?

LI'L BIT

My bra strap?—

PECK

—Li'l Bit. What's the most important thing to have control of on the inside of the car?

LI'L BIT

That's easy. The radio. I tune the radio from Mama's old fart tunes to—

(Li'l Bit turns the radio up so we can hear a 1960s tune. With surprising firmness, Peck commands:)

PECK

—Radio off. Right now. *(Li'l Bit turns the radio off)* When you are driving your car, with your license, you can fiddle with the stations all you want. But when you are driving with a learner's permit in my car, I want all your attention to be on the road.

LI'L BIT

Yes, sir.

PECK

Okay. Now the seat—forward and up. *(Li'l Bit pushes it forward)* Do you want a cushion?

LI'L BIT

No—I'm good.

PECK

You should be able to reach all the switches and controls. Your feet should be able to push the accelerator, brake and clutch all the way down. Can you do that?

LI'L BIT

Yes.

PECK

Okay, the side mirrors. You want to be able to see just a bit of the right side of the car in the right mirror—can you?

LI'L BIT

Turn it out more.

PECK

Okay. How's that?

LI'L BIT

A little more. . . . Okay, that's good.

PECK

Now the left—again, you want to be able to see behind you—but the left lane—adjust it until you feel comfortable. *(Li'l Bit does so)* Next. I want you to check the rearview mirror. Angle it so you have a clear vision of the back. *(Li'l Bit does so)* Okay. Lock your door. Make sure all the doors are locked.

LI'L BIT

(Making a joke of it) But then I'm locked in with you.

PECK

Don't fool.

LI'L BIT

All right. We're locked in.

PECK

We'll deal with the air vents and defroster later. I'm teaching you on a manual—once you learn manual, you can drive anything. I want you to be able to drive any car, any machine. Manual gives you *control*. In ice, if your brakes fail, if you need more power—okay? It's a little harder at first, but then it becomes like breathing. Now. Put your hands on the wheel. I never want to see you driving with one hand. Always two hands. *(Li'l Bit hesitates)* What? What is it now?

LI'L BIT

If I put my hands on the wheel—how do I defend myself?

PECK

(Softly) Now listen. Listen up close. We're not going to fool around with this. This is serious business. I will never touch you when you are driving a car. Understand?

LI'L BIT

Okay.

PECK

Hands on the nine o'clock and three o'clock position gives you maximum control and turn.

(Peck goes silent for a while. Li'l Bit waits for more instruction)

Okay. Just relax and listen to me, Li'l Bit, okay? I want you to lift your hands for a second and look at them. *(Li'l Bit feels a bit silly, but does it)*

Those are your two hands. When you are driving, your life is in your own two hands. Understand? *(Li'l Bit nods)*

I don't have any sons. You're the nearest to a son I'll ever have—and I want to give you something. Something that really matters to me.

There's something about driving—when you're in control of the car, just you and the machine and the road—that nobody can take from you. A power. I feel more myself in my car than anywhere else. And that's what I want to give to you.

There's a lot of assholes out there. Crazy men, arrogant idiots, drunks, angry kids, geezers who are blind—and you have to be ready for them. I want to teach you to drive like a man.

LI'L BIT

What does that mean?

PECK

Men are taught to drive with confidence—with aggression. The road belongs to them. They drive defensively—always looking out for the other guy. Women tend to be polite—to hesitate. And that can be fatal.

You're going to learn to think what the other guy is going to do before he does it. If there's an accident, and ten cars pile up, and people get killed, you're the one who's gonna steer through it, put your foot on the gas if you have to, and be the only one to walk away. I don't know how long you or I are going to live, but we're for damned sure not going to die in a car.

So if you're going to drive with me, I want you to take this very seriously.

LI'L BIT

I will, Uncle Peck. I want you to teach me to drive.

PECK

Good. You're going to pass your test on the first try. Perfect score. Before the next four weeks are over, you're going to know this baby inside and out. Treat her with respect.

LI'L BIT

Why is it a "she?"

PECK

Good question. It doesn't have to be a "she"—but when you close your eyes and think of someone who responds to your touch—someone who performs just for you and gives you what you ask for—I guess I always see a "she." You can call her what you like.

LI'L BIT

(To the audience) I closed my eyes—and decided not to change the gender.

(A Voice:)

Defensive driving involves defending yourself from hazardous and sudden changes in your automotive environment. By thinking ahead, the defensive driver can adjust to weather, road conditions and road kill. Good defensive driving involves mental and physical preparation. Are you prepared?

(Another Voice chimes in:)

You and the Reverse Gear.

LI'L BIT

1966. The Anthropology of the Female Body in Ninth Grade—
Or A Walk Down Mammary Lane.

*(Throughout the following, there is occasional rhythmic beep-
ing, like a transmitter signalling. Li'l Bit is aware of it, but
can't figure out where it is coming from. No one else seems to
hear it.)*

MALE GREEK CHORUS

In the hallway of Francis Scott Key Middle School.

*(A bell rings; the Greek Chorus is changing classes and meets
in the hall, conspiratorially.)*

TEENAGE GREEK CHORUS

She's coming!

*(Li'l Bit enters the scene; the Male Greek Chorus member has
a sudden, violent sneezing and lethal allergy attack.)*

FEMALE GREEK CHORUS

Jerome? Jerome? Are you all right?

MALE GREEK CHORUS

I—don't—know. I can't breathe—get Li'l Bit—

TEENAGE GREEK CHORUS

—He needs oxygen! —

FEMALE GREEK CHORUS

—Can you help us here?

LI'L BIT

What's wrong? Do you want me to get the school nurse—

*(The Male Greek Chorus member wheezes, grabs his throat
and sniffs at Li'l Bit's chest, which is beeping away.)*

MALE GREEK CHORUS

No—it's okay—I only get this way when I'm around an allergy trigger—

LI'L BIT

Golly. What are you allergic to?

MALE GREEK CHORUS

(With a sudden grab of her breast) Foam rubber.

(The Greek Chorus members break up with hilarity; Jerome leaps away from Li'l Bit's kicking rage with agility; as he retreats:)

LI'L BIT

Jerome! Creep! Cretin! Cro-Magnon!

TEENAGE GREEK CHORUS

Rage is not attractive in a girl.

FEMALE GREEK CHORUS

Really. Get a Sense of Humor.

(A Voice echoes:)

Good defensive driving involves mental and physical preparation. Were You Prepared?

FEMALE GREEK CHORUS

Gym Class: In the showers.

(The sudden sound of water; the Female Greek Chorus members and Li'l Bit, while fully clothed, drape towels across their fronts, miming nudity. They stand, hesitate, at an imaginary shower's edge.)

LI'L BIT

Water looks hot.

FEMALE GREEK CHORUS

Yesss. . . .

(Female Greek Chorus members are not going to make the first move. One dips a tentative toe under the water, clutching the towel around her.)

LI'L BIT

Well, I guess we'd better shower and get out of here.

FEMALE GREEK CHORUS

Yep. You go ahead. I'm still cooling off.

LI'L BIT

Okay. —Sally? Are you gonna shower?

TEENAGE GREEK CHORUS

After you—

(Li'l Bit takes a deep breath for courage, drops the towel and plunges in: The two Female Greek Chorus members look at Li'l Bit in the all together, laugh, gasp and high-five each other.)

TEENAGE GREEK CHORUS

Oh my god! Can you believe—

FEMALE GREEK CHORUS

Told you! It's not foam rubber! I win! Jerome owes me fifty cents!

(A Voice editorializes:)

Were You Prepared?

(Li'l Bit tries to cover up; she is exposed, as suddenly 1960s Motown fills the room and we segue into:)

FEMALE GREEK CHORUS
The Sock Hop.

(Li'l Bit stands up against the wall with her female classmates. Teenage Greek Chorus is mesmerized by the music and just sways alone, lip-synching the lyrics.)

LI'L BIT
I don't know. Maybe it's just me—but—do you ever feel like you're just a walking Mary Jane joke?

FEMALE GREEK CHORUS
I don't know what you mean.

LI'L BIT
You haven't heard the Mary Jane jokes? *(Female Greek Chorus member shakes her head no)* Okay. "Little Mary Jane is walking through the woods, when all of a sudden this man who was hiding behind a tree *jumps* out, *rips* open Mary Jane's blouse, and *plunges* his hands on her breasts. And Little Mary Jane just laughed and laughed because she knew her money was in her shoes."

(Li'l Bit laughs; the Female Greek Chorus does not.)

FEMALE GREEK CHORUS
You're weird.

(In another space, in a strange light, Uncle Peck stands and stares at Li'l Bit's body. He is setting up a tripod, but he just stands, appreciative, watching her.)

LI'L BIT
Well, don't you ever feel . . . self-conscious? Like you're being looked at all the time?

FEMALE GREEK CHORUS
That's not a problem for me. —Oh—look—Greg's coming over to ask you to dance.

(Teenage Greek Chorus becomes attentive, flustered. Male Greek Chorus member, as Greg, bends slightly as a very short young man, whose head is at Li'l Bit's chest level. Ardent, sincere and socially inept, Greg will become a successful gynecologist.)

TEENAGE GREEK CHORUS
(Softly) Hi, Greg.

(Greg does not hear. He is intent on only one thing.)

MALE GREEK CHORUS
(As Greg, to Li'l Bit) Good Evening. Would you care to dance?

LI'L BIT
(Gently) Thank you very much, Greg—but I'm going to sit this one out.

MALE GREEK CHORUS
(As Greg) Oh. Okay. I'll try my luck later.

(He disappears.)

TEENAGE GREEK CHORUS
Oohhh.

(Li'l Bit relaxes. Then she tenses, aware of Peck's gaze.)

FEMALE GREEK CHORUS
Take pity on him. Someone should.

LI'L BIT
But he's so short.

TEENAGE GREEK CHORUS
He can't help it.

LI'L BIT
But his head comes up to *(Li'l Bit gestures)* here. And I think he asks me on the fast dances so he can watch me—you know—jiggle.

FEMALE GREEK CHORUS
I wish I had your problems.

(The tune changes; Greg is across the room in a flash.)

MALE GREEK CHORUS
(As Greg) Evening again. May I ask you for the honor of a spin on the floor?

LI'L BIT
I'm . . . very complimented, Greg. But I . . . I just don't do fast dances.

MALE GREEK CHORUS
(As Greg) Oh. No problem. That's okay.

(He disappears. Teenage Greek Chorus watches him go.)

TEENAGE GREEK CHORUS
That is just so—*sad.*

(Li'l Bit becomes aware of Peck waiting.)

FEMALE GREEK CHORUS
You know, you should take it as a compliment that the guys want to watch you jiggle. They're guys. That's what they're supposed to do.

LI'L BIT
I guess you're right. But sometimes I feel like these alien life forces, these two mounds of flesh have grafted themselves onto my chest, and they're using me until they can "propagate" and take over the world and they'll just keep growing, with a mind of their own until I collapse under their weight and they suck all the nourishment out of my body and I finally just waste away while they get bigger and bigger and— *(Li'l Bit's classmates are just staring at her in disbelief)*

FEMALE GREEK CHORUS

—You are the strangest girl I have ever met.

(Li'l Bit's trying to joke but feels on the verge of tears.)

LI'L BIT

Or maybe someone's implanted radio transmitters in my chest at a frequency I can't hear, that girls can't detect, but they're sending out these signals to men who get mesmerized, like sirens, calling them to dash themselves on these "rocks"—

(Just then, the music segues into a slow dance, perhaps a Beach Boys tune like "Little Surfer," but over the music there's a rhythmic, hypnotic beeping transmitted, which both Greg and Peck hear. Li'l Bit hears it too, and in horror she stares at her chest. She, too, is almost hypnotized. In a trance, Greg responds to the signals and is called to her side—actually, her front. Like a zombie, he stands in front of her, his eyes planted on her two orbs.)

MALE GREEK CHORUS

(As Greg) This one's a slow dance. I hope your dance card isn't . . . filled?

(Li'l Bit is aware of Peck; but the signals are calling her to him. The signals are no longer transmitters, but an electromagnetic force, pulling Li'l Bit to his side, where he again waits for her to join him. She must get away from the dance floor.)

LI'L BIT

Greg—you really are a nice boy. But I don't like to dance.

MALE GREEK CHORUS

(As Greg) That's okay. We don't have to move or anything. I could just hold you and we could just *sway* a little—

LI'L BIT

— No! I'm sorry—but I think I have to leave; I hear someone calling me—

(Li'l Bit starts across the dance floor, leaving Greg behind. The beeping stops. The lights change, although the music does not. As Li'l Bit talks to the audience, she continues to change and prepare for the coming session. She should be wearing a tight tank top or a sheer blouse and very tight pants. To the audience:)

In every man's home some small room, some zone in his house, is set aside. It might be the attic, or the study, or a den. And there's an invisible sign as if from the old treehouse: Girls Keep Out.

Here, away from female eyes, lace doilies and crochet, he keeps his manly toys: the Vargas pinups, the tackle. A scent of tobacco and WD-40. *(She inhales deeply)* A dash of his Bay Rum. Ahhh . . . *(Li'l Bit savors it for just a moment more)*

Here he keeps his secrets: a violin or saxophone, drum set or darkroom, and the stacks of *Playboy*. *(In a whisper)* Here, in my aunt's home, it was the basement. Uncle Peck's turf.

(A Voice commands:)

You and the Reverse Gear.

LI'L BIT

1965. The Photo Shoot.

(Li'l Bit steps into the scene as a nervous but curious thirteen year old. Music, from the previous scene, continues to play, changing into something like Roy Orbison later—something seductive with a beat. Peck fiddles, all business, with his camera. As in the driving lesson, he is all competency and concentration. Li'l Bit stands awkwardly. He looks through the Leica camera on the tripod, adjusts the back lighting, etc.)

PECK

Are you cold? The lights should heat up some in a few minutes—

LI'L BIT

—Aunt Mary is?

PECK

At the National Theatre matinee. With your mother. We have time.

LI'L BIT

But—what if—

PECK

—And so what if they return? I told them you and I were going to be working with my camera. They won't come down. *(Li'l Bit is quiet, apprehensive)* —Look, are you sure you want to do this?

LI'L BIT

I said I'd do it. But—

PECK

—I know. You've drawn the line.

LI'L BIT

(Reassured) That's right. No frontal nudity.

PECK

Good heavens, girl, where did you pick that up?

LI'L BIT

(Defensive) I *read.*

(Peck tries not to laugh.)

PECK

And I read *Playboy* for the interviews. Okay. Let's try some different music.

(Peck goes to an expensive reel-to-reel and forwards. Something like "Sweet Dreams" begins to play.)

LI'L BIT

I didn't know you listened to this.

PECK

I'm not dead, you know. I try to keep up. Do you like this song? *(Li'l Bit nods with pleasure)* Good. Now listen—at professional photo shoots, they always play music for the models. Okay? I want you to just enjoy the music. Listen to it with your body, and just—respond.

LI'L BIT

Respond to the music with my . . . body?

PECK

Right. Almost like dancing. Here—let's get you on the stool, first. *(Peck comes over and helps her up)*

LI'L BIT

But nothing showing—

(Peck firmly, with his large capable hands, brushes back her hair, angles her face. Li'l Bit turns to him like a plant to the sun.)

PECK

Nothing showing. Just a peek.
    (He holds her by the shoulder, looking at her critically. Then he unbuttons her blouse to the midpoint, and runs his hands over the flesh of her exposed sternum, arranging the fabric, just touching her. Deliberately, calmly. Asexually. Li'l Bit quiets, sits perfectly still, and closes her eyes)
    Okay?

LI'L BIT

Yes.

(Peck goes back to his camera.)

PECK

I'm going to keep talking to you. Listen without responding to what I'm saying; you want to *listen* to the music. Sway, move just your torso or your head—I've got to check the light meter.

LI'L BIT

But—you'll be watching.

PECK

No—I'm not here—just my voice. Pretend you're in your room all alone on a Friday night with your mirror—and the music feels good—just move for me, Li'l Bit—

(Li'l Bit closes her eyes. At first self-conscious; then she gets more into the music and begins to sway. We hear the camera start to whir. Throughout the shoot, there can be a slide montage of actual shots of the actor playing Li'l Bit—interspersed with other models à la Playboy, Calvin Klein *and* Victoriana/Lewis Carroll's Alice Liddell)

That's it. That looks great. Okay. Just keep doing that. Lift your head up a bit more, good, good, just keep moving, that a girl—you're a very beautiful young woman. Do you know that? *(Li'l Bit looks up, blushes. Peck shoots the camera. The audience should see this shot on the screen)*

LI'L BIT

No. I don't know that.

PECK

Listen to the music. *(Li'l Bit closes her eyes again)* Well you are. For a thirteen year old, you have a body a twenty-year-old woman would die for.

LI'L BIT

The boys in school don't think so.

PECK

The boys in school are little Neanderthals in short pants. You're ten years ahead of them in maturity; it's gonna take a while for them to catch up.

(Peck clicks another shot; we see a faint smile on Li'l Bit on the screen)

Girls turn into women long before boys turn into men.

LI'L BIT
Why is that?

PECK

I don't know, Li'l Bit. But it's a blessing for men.
(Li'l Bit turns silent) Keep moving. Try arching your back
on the stool, hands behind you, and throw your head back.
(The slide shows a Playboy *model in this pose)* Oohh, great.
That one was great. Turn your head away, same position.
(Whir) Beautiful.

(Li'l Bit looks at him a bit defiantly.)

LI'L BIT

I think Aunt Mary is beautiful.

(Peck stands still.)

PECK

My wife is a very beautiful woman. Her beauty doesn't cancel
yours out. *(More casually; he returns to the camera)* All the
women in your family are beautiful. In fact, I think all women
are. You're not listening to the music. *(Peck shoots some more
film in silence)* All right, turn your head to the left. Good. Now
take the back of your right hand and put in on your right
cheek—your elbow angled up—now slowly, slowly, stroke
your cheek, draw back your hair with the back of your hand.
(Another classic Playboy *or* Vargas) Good. One hand above
and behind your head; stretch your body; smile. *(Another pose)*
    Li'l Bit. I want you to think of something that makes you
laugh—

LI'L BIT

I can't think of anything.

PECK

Okay. Think of Big Papa chasing Grandma around the living
room. *(Li'l Bit lifts her head and laughs. Click. We should see*

this shot) Good. Both hands behind your head. Great! Hold that. *(From behind his camera)* You're doing great work. If we keep this up, in five years we'll have a really professional portfolio.

(Li'l Bit stops.)

LI'L BIT
What do you mean in five years?

PECK
You can't submit work to *Playboy* until you're eighteen.—

(Peck continues to shoot; he knows he's made a mistake.)

LI'L BIT
—Wait a minute. You're joking, aren't you, Uncle Peck?

PECK
Heck, no. You can't get into *Playboy* unless you're the very best. And you are the very best.

LI'L BIT
I would never do that!

(Peck stops shooting. He turns off the music.)

PECK
Why? There's nothing wrong with *Playboy*—it's a very classy maga—

LI'L BIT
(More upset) But I thought you said I should go to college!

PECK
Wait—Li'l Bit—it's nothing like that. Very respectable women model for *Playboy*—actresses with major careers—women in college—there's an Ivy League issue every—

LI'L BIT

—I'm never doing anything like that! You'd show other people these—other *men*—these—what I'm doing. —Why would you do that?! Any *boy* around here could just pick up, just go into The Stop & Go and *buy*— Why would you ever want to—to share—

PECK

—Whoa, whoa. Just stop a second and listen to me. Li'l Bit. Listen. There's nothing wrong in what we're doing. I'm very proud of you. I think you have a wonderful body and an even more wonderful mind. And of course I want other people to *appreciate* it. It's not anything shameful.

LI'L BIT

(Hurt) But this is something—that I'm only doing for you. This is something—that you said was just between us.

PECK

It is. And if that's how you feel, five years from now, it will remain that way. Okay? I know you're not going to do anything you don't feel like doing.

(He walks back to the camera) Do you want to stop now? I've got just a few more shots on this roll—

LI'L BIT

I don't want anyone seeing this.

PECK

I swear to you. No one will. I'll treasure this—that you're doing this only for me.

(Li'l Bit, still shaken, sits on the stool. She closes her eyes) Li'l Bit? Open your eyes and look at me. *(Li'l Bit shakes her head no)* Come on. Just open your eyes, honey.

LI'L BIT

If I look at you—if I look at the camera: You're gonna know what I'm thinking. You'll see right through me—

PECK

—No, I won't. I want you to look at me. All right, then. I just want you to listen. Li'l Bit. *(She waits)* I love you. *(Li'l Bit opens her eyes; she is startled. Peck captures the shot. On the screen we see right though her. Peck says softly)* Do you know that? *(Li'l Bit nods her head yes)* I have loved you every day since the day you were born.

LI'L BIT

Yes.

(Li'l Bit and Peck just look at each other. Beat. Beneath the shot of herself on the screen, Li'l Bit, still looking at her uncle, begins to unbutton her blouse.

A neutral Voice cuts off the above scene with:)

Implied Consent.
As an individual operating a motor vehicle in the state of Maryland, you must abide by "Implied Consent." If you do not consent to take the blood alcohol content test, there may be severe penalties: a suspension of license, a fine, community service and a possible *jail* sentence.

(The Voice shifts tone:)

Idling in the Neutral Gear.

MALE GREEK CHORUS

(Announcing) Aunt Mary on behalf of her husband.

(Female Greek Chorus checks her appearance, and with dignity comes to the front of the stage and sits down to talk to the audience.)

FEMALE GREEK CHORUS

(As Aunt Mary) My husband was such a good man—is. Is such a good man. Every night, he does the dishes. The second he comes home, he's taking out the garbage, or doing yard

work, lifting the heavy things I can't. Everyone in the neighborhood borrows Peck—it's true—women with husbands of their own, men who just don't have Peck's abilities—there's always a knock on our door for a jump start on cold mornings, when anyone needs a ride, or help shoveling the sidewalk—I look out, and there Peck is, without a coat, pitching in.

I know I'm lucky. The man works from dawn to dusk. And the overtime he does every year—my poor sister. She sits every Christmas when I come to dinner with a new stole, or diamonds, or with the tickets to Bermuda.

I know he has troubles. And we don't talk about them. I wonder, sometimes, what happened to him during the war. The men who fought World War II didn't have "rap sessions" to talk about their feelings. Men in his generation were expected to be quiet about it and get on with their lives. And sometimes I can feel him just fighting the trouble—whatever has burrowed deeper than the scar tissue—and we don't talk about it. I know he's having a bad spell because he comes looking for me in the house, and just hangs around me until it passes. And I keep my banter light—I discuss a new recipe, or sales, or gossip—because I think domesticity can be a balm for men when they're lost. We sit in the house and listen to the peace of the clock ticking in his well-ordered living room, until it passes.

(Sharply) I'm not a fool. I know what's going on. I wish you could feel how hard Peck fights against it—he's swimming against the tide, and what he needs is to see me on the shore, believing in him, knowing he won't go under, he won't give up—

And I want to say this about my niece. She's a sly one, that one is. She knows exactly what she's doing; she's twisted Peck around her little finger and thinks it's all a big secret. Yet another one who's borrowing my husband until it doesn't suit her anymore.

Well. I'm counting the days until she goes away to school. And she manipulates someone else. And then he'll come back again, and sit in the kitchen while I bake, or beside me on the sofa when I sew in the evenings. I'm a very patient woman. But I'd like my husband back.

I am counting the days.

(A Voice repeats:)

You and the Reverse Gear.

MALE GREEK CHORUS
Li'l Bit's Thirteenth Christmas. Uncle Peck Does the Dishes.
Christmas 1964.

*(Peck stands in a dress shirt and tie, nice pants, with an apron.
He is washing dishes. He's in a mood we haven't seen. Quiet,
brooding. Li'l Bit watches him a moment before seeking him
out.)*

LI'L BIT
Uncle Peck? *(He does not answer. He continues to work on
the pots)* I didn't know where you'd gone to. *(He nods. She
takes this as a sign to come in)* Don't you want to sit with us
for a while?

PECK
No. I'd rather do the dishes.

(Pause. Li'l Bit watches him.)

LI'L BIT
You're the only man I know who does dishes. *(Peck says nothing)* I think it's really nice.

PECK
My wife has been on her feet all day. So's your grandmother
and your mother.

LI'L BIT
I know. *(Beat)* Do you want some help?

PECK
No. *(He softens a bit towards her)* You can help by just talking to me.

LI'L BIT

Big Papa never does the dishes. I think it's nice.

PECK

I think men should be nice to women. Women are always working for us. There's nothing particularly manly in wolfing down food and then sitting around in a stupor while the women clean up.

LI'L BIT

That looks like a really neat camera that Aunt Mary got you.

PECK

It is. It's a very nice one.

(Pause, as Peck works on the dishes and some demon that Li'l Bit intuits.)

LI'L BIT

Did Big Papa hurt your feelings?

PECK

(Tired) What? Oh, no—it doesn't hurt me. Family is family. I'd rather have him picking on me than—I don't pay him any mind, Li'l Bit.

LI'L BIT

Are you angry with us?

PECK

No, Li'l Bit. I'm not angry.

(Another pause.)

LI'L BIT

We missed you at Thanksgiving. . . . I did. I missed you.

PECK

Well, there were . . . "things" going on. I didn't want to spoil anyone's Thanksgiving.

LI'L BIT

Uncle Peck? *(Very carefully)* Please don't drink anymore tonight.

PECK

I'm not . . . overdoing it.

LI'L BIT

I know. *(Beat)* Why do you drink so much?

(Peck stops and thinks, carefully.)

PECK

Well, Li'l Bit—let me explain it this way. There are some people who have a . . . a "fire" in the belly. I think they go to work on Wall Street or they run for office. And then there are people who have a "fire" in their heads—and they become writers or scientists or historians. *(He smiles a little at her)* You. You've got a "fire" in the head. And then there are people like me.

LI'L BIT

Where do you have . . . a fire?

PECK

I have a fire in my heart. And sometimes the drinking helps.

LI'L BIT

There's got to be other things that can help.

PECK

I suppose there are.

LI'L BIT

Does it help—to talk to me?

PECK

Yes. It does. *(Quiet)* I don't get to see you very much.

LI'L BIT

I know. *(Li'l Bit thinks)* You could talk to me more.

PECK

Oh?

LI'L BIT

I could make a deal with you, Uncle Peck.

PECK

I'm listening.

LI'L BIT

We could meet and talk—once a week. You could just store up whatever's bothering you during the week—and then we could talk.

PECK

Would you like that?

LI'L BIT

As long as you don't drink. I'd meet you somewhere for lunch or for a walk—on the weekends—as long as you stop drinking. And we could talk about whatever you want.

PECK

You would do that for me?

LI'L BIT

I don't think I'd want Mom to know. Or Aunt Mary. I wouldn't want them to think—

PECK

—No. It would just be us talking.

LI'L BIT

I'll tell Mom I'm going to a girlfriend's. To study. Mom doesn't get home until six, so you can call me after school and tell me where to meet you.

PECK

You get home at four?

LI'L BIT

We can meet once a week. But only in public. You've got to let me—draw the line. And once it's drawn, you mustn't cross it.

PECK

Understood.

LI'L BIT

Would that help?

(Peck is very moved.)

PECK

Yes. Very much.

LI'L BIT

I'm going to join the others in the living room now. *(Li'l Bit turns to go)*

PECK

Merry Christmas, Li'l Bit.

(Li'l Bit bestows a very warm smile on him.)

LI'L BIT

Merry Christmas, Uncle Peck.

(A Voice dictates:)

Shifting Forward from Second to Third Gear.

(The Male and Female Greek Chorus members come forward.)

MALE GREEK CHORUS
1969. Days and Gifts: A Countdown:

FEMALE GREEK CHORUS
A note. "September 3, 1969. Li'l Bit: You've only been away two days and it feels like months. Hope your dorm room is cozy. I'm sending you this tape cassette—it's a new model— so you'll have some music in your room. Also that music you're reading about for class—*Carmina Burana.* Hope you enjoy. Only ninety days to go! —Peck."

MALE GREEK CHORUS
September 22. A bouquet of roses. A note: "Miss you like crazy. Sixty-nine days . . ."

TEENAGE GREEK CHORUS
September 25. A box of chocolates. A card: "Don't worry about the weight gain. You still look great. Got a post office box—write to me there. Sixty-six days. —Love, your candy man."

MALE GREEK CHORUS
October 16. A note: "Am trying to get through the Jane Austin you're reading—*Emma*—here's a book in return: *Liaisons Dangereuses.* Hope you're saving time for me." Scrawled in the margin the number: "47."

FEMALE GREEK CHORUS
November 16. "Sixteen days to go! —Hope you like the perfume. —Having a hard time reaching you on the dorm phone. You must be in the library a lot. Won't you think about me getting you your own phone so we can talk?"

TEENAGE GREEK CHORUS
November 18. "Li'l Bit—got a package returned to the P.O. Box. Have you changed dorms? Call me at work or write to

the P.O. Am still on the wagon. Waiting to see you. Only two weeks more!"

MALE GREEK CHORUS

November 23. A letter. "Li'l Bit. So disappointed you couldn't come home for the turkey. Sending you some money for a nice dinner out—nine days and counting!"

GREEK CHORUS

(In unison) November 25th. A letter:

LI'L BIT

"Dear Uncle Peck: I am sending this to you at work. Don't come up next weekend for my birthday. I will not be here —"

(A Voice directs:)

Shifting Forward from Third to Fourth Gear.

MALE GREEK CHORUS

December 10, 1969. A hotel room. Philadelphia. There is no moon tonight.

(Peck sits on the side of the bed while Li'l Bit paces. He can't believe she's in his room, but there's a desperate edge to his happiness. Li'l Bit is furious, edgy. There is a bottle of champagne in an ice bucket in a very nice hotel room.)

PECK

Why don't you sit?

LI'L BIT

I don't want to. —What's the champagne for?

PECK

I thought we might toast your birthday—

LI'L BIT

—I am so pissed off at you, Uncle Peck.

PECK

Why?

LI'L BIT

I mean, are you crazy?

PECK

What did I do?

LI'L BIT

You scared the holy crap out of me—sending me that stuff in the mail—

PECK

—They were gifts! I just wanted to give you some little perks your first semester—

LI'L BIT

—Well, what the hell were those numbers all about! Forty-four days to go—only two more weeks. —And then just numbers—69—68—67—like some serial killer!

PECK

Li'l Bit! Whoa! This is me you're talking to—I was just trying to pick up your spirits, trying to celebrate your birthday.

LI'L BIT

My *eighteenth* birthday. I'm not a child, Uncle Peck. You were counting down to my eighteenth birthday.

PECK

So?

LI'L BIT

So? So statutory rape is not in effect when a young woman turns eighteen. And you and I both know it.

(Peck is walking on ice.)

PECK

I think you misunderstand.

LI'L BIT

I think I understand all too well. I know what you want to do five steps ahead of you doing it. Defensive Driving 101.

PECK

Then why did you suggest we meet here instead of the restaurant?

LI'L BIT

I don't want to have this conversation in public.

PECK

Fine. Fine. We have a lot to talk about.

LI'L BIT

Yeah. We do.
 (Li'l Bit doesn't want to do what she has to do) Could I . . . have some of that champagne?

PECK

Of course, madam! *(Peck makes a big show of it)* Let me do the honors. I wasn't sure which you might prefer—Taittingers or Veuve Clicquot—so I thought we'd start out with an old standard—Perrier Jouet. *(The bottle is popped)*
 Quick—Li'l Bit—your glass! *(Uncle Peck fills Li'l Bit's glass. He puts the bottle back in the ice and goes for a can of ginger ale)* Let me get some of this ginger ale—my bubbly— and toast you.

(He turns and sees that Li'l Bit has not waited for him.)

LI'L BIT

Oh—sorry, Uncle Peck. Let me have another. *(Peck fills her glass and reaches for his ginger ale; she stops him)* Uncle Peck—maybe you should join me in the champagne.

PECK

You want me to—drink?

LI'L BIT

It's not polite to let a lady drink alone.

PECK

Well, missy, if you insist. . . . *(Peck hesitates)* —Just one. It's been a while. *(Peck fills another flute for himself)* There. I'd like to propose a toast to you and your birthday! *(Peck sips it tentatively)* I'm not used to this anymore.

LI'L BIT

You don't have anywhere to go tonight, do you?

(Peck hopes this is a good sign.)

PECK

I'm all yours. —God, it's good to see you! I've gotten so used to . . . to . . . talking to you in my head. I'm used to seeing you every week—there's so much—I don't quite know where to begin. How's school, Li'l Bit?

LI'L BIT

I—it's hard. Uncle Peck. Harder than I thought it would be. I'm in the middle of exams and papers and—I don't know.

PECK

You'll pull through. You always do.

LI'L BIT

Maybe. I . . . might be flunking out.

PECK

You always think the worse, Li'l Bit, but when the going gets tough— *(Li'l Bit shrugs and pours herself another glass)* —Hey, honey, go easy on that stuff, okay?

LI'L BIT

Is it very expensive?

PECK

Only the best for you. But the cost doesn't matter—champagne should be "sipped." *(Li'l Bit is quiet)* Look—if you're in trouble in school—you can always come back home for a while.

LI'L BIT

No— *(Li'l Bit tries not to be so harsh)* —Thanks, Uncle Peck, but I'll figure some way out of this.

PECK

You're supposed to get in scrapes, your first year away from home.

LI'L BIT

Right. How's Aunt Mary?

PECK

She's fine. *(Pause)* Well—how about the new car?

LI'L BIT

It's real nice. What is it, again?

PECK

It's a Cadillac El Dorado.

LI'L BIT

Oh. Well, I'm real happy for you, Uncle Peck.

PECK

I got it for you.

LI'L BIT

What?

PECK

I always wanted to get a Cadillac—but I thought, Peck, wait until Li'l Bit's old enough—and thought maybe you'd like to drive it, too.

LI'L BIT

(Confused) Why would I want to drive your car?

PECK

Just because it's the best—I want you to have the best.

(They are running out of "gas"; small talk.)

| **LI'L BIT** | **PECK** |
| Listen, Uncle Peck, I don't know how to begin this, but— | I have been thinking of how to say this in my head, over and over— |

PECK

Sorry.

LI'L BIT

You first.

PECK

Well, your going away—has just made me realize how much I miss you. Talking to you and being alone with you. I've really come to depend on you, Li'l Bit. And it's been so hard to get in touch with you lately—the distance and—and you're never in when I call—I guess you've been living in the library—

LI'L BIT

—No—the problem is, I haven't been in the library—

PECK

—Well, it doesn't matter—I hope you've been missing me as much.

LI'L BIT

Uncle Peck—I've been thinking a lot about this—and I came here tonight to tell you that—I'm not doing very well. I'm getting very confused—I can't concentrate on my work—and now that I'm away—I've been going over and over it in my mind—and I don't want us to "see" each other anymore. Other than with the rest of the family.

PECK

(Quiet) Are you seeing other men?

LI'L BIT

(Getting agitated) I—no, that's not the reason—I—well, yes, I am seeing other—listen, it's not really anybody's business!

PECK

Are you in love with anyone else?

LI'L BIT

That's not what this is about.

PECK

Li'l Bit—you're scared. Your mother and your grandparents have filled your head with all kinds of nonsense about men— I hear them working on you all the time—and you're scared. It won't hurt you—if the man you go to bed with really loves you. *(Li'l Bit is scared. She starts to tremble)* And I have loved you since the day I held you in my hand. And I think everyone's just gotten you frightened to death about something that is just like breathing—

LI'L BIT

Oh, my god—*(She takes a breath)* I can't see you anymore, Uncle Peck.

(Peck downs the rest of his champagne.)

PECK

Li'l Bit. Listen. Listen. Open your eyes and look at me. Come on. Just open your eyes, honey. *(Li'l Bit, eyes squeezed shut, refuses)* All right then. I just want you to listen. Li'l Bit—I'm going to ask you just this once. Of your own free will. Just lie down on the bed with me—our clothes on—just lie down with me, a man and a woman . . . and let's . . . hold one another. Nothing else. Before you say anything else. I want the chance to . . . hold you. Because sometimes the body knows things that the mind isn't listening to . . . and after I've held you, then I want you to tell me what you feel.

LI'L BIT

You'll just . . . hold me?

PECK

Yes. And then you can tell me what you're feeling.

(Li'l Bit—half wanting to run, half wanting to get it over with, half wanting to be held by him:)

LI'L BIT

Yes. All right. Just hold. Nothing else.

(Peck lies down on the bed and holds his arms out to her. Li'l Bit lies beside him, putting her head on his chest. He looks as if he's trying to soak her into his pores by osmosis. He strokes her hair, and she lies very still. The Male Greek Chorus member and the Female Greek Chorus member as Aunt Mary come into the room.)

MALE GREEK CHORUS

Recipe for a Southern Boy:

FEMALE GREEK CHORUS

(As Aunt Mary) A drawl of molasses in the way he speaks.

MALE GREEK CHORUS

A gumbo of red and brown mixed in the cream of his skin.

(While Peck lies, his eyes closed, Li'l Bit rises in the bed and responds to her aunt.)

LI'L BIT

Warm brown eyes—

FEMALE GREEK CHORUS

(As Aunt Mary) Bedroom eyes—

MALE GREEK CHORUS

A dash of Southern Baptist Fire and Brimstone—

LI'L BIT

A curl of Elvis on his forehead—

FEMALE GREEK CHORUS

(As Aunt Mary) A splash of Bay Rum—

MALE GREEK CHORUS

A closely shaven beard that he razors just for you—

FEMALE GREEK CHORUS

(As Aunt Mary) Large hands—rough hands—

LI'L BIT

Warm hands—

MALE GREEK CHORUS

The steel of the military in his walk —

LI'L BIT

The slouch of the fishing skiff in his walk —

MALE GREEK CHORUS

Neatly pressed khakis—

FEMALE GREEK CHORUS

(As Aunt Mary) And under the wide leather of the belt —

LI'L BIT

Sweat of cypress and sand —

MALE GREEK CHORUS

Neatly pressed khakis—

LI'L BIT

His heart beating Dixie—

FEMALE GREEK CHORUS

(As Aunt Mary) The whisper of the zipper—you could reach out with your hand and—

LI'L BIT

His mouth—

FEMALE GREEK CHORUS

(As Aunt Mary) You could just reach out and—

LI'L BIT

Hold him in your hand—

FEMALE GREEK CHORUS

(As Aunt Mary) And his mouth—

(Li'l Bit rises above her uncle and looks at his mouth; she starts to lower herself to kiss him—and wrenches herself free. She gets up from the bed.)

LI'L BIT

—I've got to get back.

PECK

Wait—Li'l Bit. Did you . . . feel nothing?

LI'L BIT

(Lying) No. Nothing.

PECK

Do you—do you think of me?

(The Greek Chorus whispers:)

FEMALE GREEK CHORUS

Khakis —

MALE GREEK CHORUS

Bay Rum —

FEMALE GREEK CHORUS

The whisper of the—

LI'L BIT

—No.

(Peck, in a rush, trembling, gets something out of his pocket.)

PECK

I'm forty-five. That's not old for a man. And I haven't been able to do anything else but think of you. I can't concentrate on my work—Li'l Bit. You've got to—I want you to think about what I am about to ask you.

LI'L BIT

I'm listening.

(Peck opens a small ring box.)

PECK

I want you to be my wife.

LI'L BIT

This isn't happening.

PECK

I'll tell Mary I want a divorce. We're not blood-related. It would be legal—

LI'L BIT

—What have you been thinking! You are married to my aunt, Uncle Peck. She's my family. You have—you have gone way over the line. Family is family.

(Quickly, Li'l Bit flies through the room, gets her coat) I'm leaving. Now. I am not seeing you. Again.

(Peck lies down on the bed for a moment, trying to absorb the terrible news. For a moment, he almost curls into a fetal position)

I'm not coming home for Christmas. You should go home to Aunt Mary. Go home now, Uncle Peck.

(Peck gets control, and sits, rigid)

Uncle Peck?—I'm sorry but I have to go.

(Pause)

Are you all right.

(With a discipline that comes from being told that boys don't cry, Peck stands upright.)

PECK

I'm fine. I just think—I need a real drink.

(The Male Greek Chorus has become a bartender. At a small counter, he is lining up shots for Peck. As Li'l Bit narrates, we see Peck sitting, carefully and calmly downing shot glasses.)

LI'L BIT

(To the audience) I never saw him again. I stayed away from Christmas and Thanksgiving for years after.

It took my uncle seven years to drink himself to death. First he lost his job, then his wife, and finally his driver's license. He retreated to his house, and had his bottles delivered.

(Peck stands, and puts his hands in front of him—almost like Superman flying)

One night he tried to go downstairs to the basement—and he flew down the steep basement stairs. My aunt came by weekly to put food on the porch, and she noticed the mail and the papers stacked up, uncollected.

They found him at the bottom of the stairs. Just steps away from his dark room.

Now that I'm old enough, there are some questions I would have liked to have asked him. Who did it to you, Uncle Peck? How old were you? Were you eleven?

(Peck moves to the driver's seat of the car and waits)

Sometimes I think of my uncle as a kind of Flying Dutchman. In the opera, the Dutchman is doomed to wander the sea; but every seven years he can come ashore, and if he finds a maiden who will love him of her own free will—he will be released.

And I see Uncle Peck in my mind, in his Chevy '56, a spirit driving up and down the back roads of Carolina—looking for a young girl who, of her own free will, will love him. Release him.

(A Voice states:)

You and the Reverse Gear.

LI'L BIT

The summer of 1962. On Men, Sex, and Women: Part III:

(Li'l Bit steps, as an eleven year old, into:)

FEMALE GREEK CHORUS

(As Mother) It is out of the question. End of Discussion.

LI'L BIT

But why?

FEMALE GREEK CHORUS

(As Mother) Li'l Bit—we are not discussing this. I said no.

LI'L BIT

But I could spend an extra week at the beach! You're not telling me why!

FEMALE GREEK CHORUS

(As Mother) Your uncle pays entirely too much attention to you.

LI'L BIT

He listens to me when I talk. And—and he talks to me. He teaches me about things. Mama—he knows an awful lot.

FEMALE GREEK CHORUS

(As Mother) He's a small town hick who's learned how to mix drinks from Hugh Hefner.

LI'L BIT

Who's Hugh Hefner?

(Beat.)

FEMALE GREEK CHORUS

(As Mother) I am not letting an eleven-year-old girl spend seven hours alone in the car with a man. . . . I don't like the way your uncle looks at you.

LI'L BIT

For god's sake, mother! Just because you've gone through a bad time with my father—you think every man is evil!

FEMALE GREEK CHORUS

(As Mother) Oh no, Li'l Bit—not all men. . . . We . . . we just haven't been very lucky with the men in our family.

LI'L BIT

Just because you lost your husband—I still deserve a chance at having a father! Someone! A man who will look out for me! Don't I get a chance?

FEMALE GREEK CHORUS

(As Mother) I will feel terrible if something happens.

LI'L BIT

Mother! It's in your head! Nothing will happen! I can take care of myself. And I can certainly handle Uncle Peck.

FEMALE GREEK CHORUS

(As Mother) All right. But I'm warning you—if anything happens, I hold you responsible.

(Li'l Bit moves out of this scene and toward the car.)

LI'L BIT

1962. On the Back Roads of Carolina: The First Driving Lesson.

(The Teenage Greek Chorus member stands apart on stage. She will speak all of Li'l Bit's lines. Li'l Bit sits beside Peck in the front seat. She looks at him closely, remembering.)

PECK

Li'l Bit? Are you getting tired?

TEENAGE GREEK CHORUS

A little.

PECK

It's a long drive. But we're making really good time. We can take the back road from here and see . . . a little scenery. Say— I've got an idea— *(Peck checks his rearview mirror)*

TEENAGE GREEK CHORUS

Are we stopping, Uncle Peck?

PECK

There's no traffic here. Do you want to drive?

TEENAGE GREEK CHORUS

I can't drive.

PECK

It's easy. I'll show you how. I started driving when I was your age. Don't you want to?—

TEENAGE GREEK CHORUS

—But it's against the law at my age!

PECK

And that's why you can't tell anyone I'm letting you do this—

TEENAGE GREEK CHORUS

—But—I can't reach the pedals.

PECK

You can sit in my lap and steer. I'll push the pedals for you. Did your father ever let you drive his car?

TEENAGE GREEK CHORUS

No way.

PECK

Want to try?

TEENAGE GREEK CHORUS

Okay. (*Li'l Bit moves into Peck's lap. She leans against him, closing her eyes*)

PECK

You're just a little thing, aren't you? Okay—now think of the wheel as a big clock—I want you to put your right hand on the clock where three o'clock would be; and your left hand on the nine—

(*Li'l Bit puts one hand to Peck's face, to stroke him. Then, she takes the wheel.*)

TEENAGE GREEK CHORUS

Am I doing it right?

PECK

That's right. Now, whatever you do, don't let go of the wheel. You tell me whether to go faster or slower—

TEENAGE GREEK CHORUS

Not so fast, Uncle Peck!

PECK

Li'l Bit—I need you to watch the road—

(Peck puts his hands on Li'l Bit's breasts. She relaxes against him, silent, accepting his touch.)

TEENAGE GREEK CHORUS

Uncle Peck—what are you doing?

PECK

Keep driving. *(He slips his hands under her blouse)*

TEENAGE GREEK CHORUS

Uncle Peck—please don't do this—

PECK

—Just a moment longer . . . *(Peck tenses against Li'l Bit)*

TEENAGE GREEK CHORUS

(Trying not to cry) This isn't happening.

(Peck tenses more, sharply. He buries his face in Li'l Bit's neck, and moans softly. The Teenage Greek Chorus exits, and Li'l Bit steps out of the car. Peck, too, disappears.
A Voice reflects:)

Driving in Today's World.

LI'L BIT

That day was the last day I lived in my body. I retreated above the neck, and I've lived inside the "fire" in my head ever since.

And now that seems like a long, long time ago. When we were both very young.

And before you know it, I'll be thirty-five. That's getting up there for a woman. And I find myself believing in things that a younger self vowed never to believe in. Things like family and forgiveness.

I know I'm lucky. Although I still have never known what it feels like to jog or dance. Any thing that . . . "jiggles." I do like to watch people on the dance floor, or out on the running paths, just jiggling away. And I say—good for them. *(Li'l Bit moves to the car with pleasure)*

The nearest sensation I feel—of flight in the body—I guess I feel when I'm driving. On a day like today. It's five A.M. The radio says it's going to be clear and crisp. I've got five hundred miles of highway ahead of me—and some back roads too. I filled the tank last night, and had the oil checked. Checked the tires, too. You've got to treat her . . . with respect.

First thing I do is: Check under the car. To see if any two year olds or household cats have crawled beneath, and strategically placed their skulls behind my back tires. *(Li'l Bit crouches)*

Nope. Then I get in the car. *(Li'l Bit does so)*

I lock the doors. And turn the key. Then I adjust the most important control on the dashboard—the radio— *(Li'l Bit turns the radio on: We hear all of the Greek Chorus overlapping, and static:)*

FEMALE GREEK CHORUS

(Overlapping) —"You were so tiny you fit in his hand—"

MALE GREEK CHORUS

(Overlapping) —"How is Shakespeare gonna help her lie on her back in the —"

TEENAGE GREEK CHORUS

(Overlapping) —"Am I doing it right?"

(Li'l Bit fine-tunes the radio station. A song like "Dedicated to the One I Love" or Orbison's "Sweet Dreams" comes on, and cuts off the Greek Chorus.)

LI'L BIT

Ahh . . . *(Beat)* I adjust my seat. Fasten my seat belt. Then I check the right side mirror—check the left side. *(She does)* Finally, I adjust the rearview mirror. *(As Li'l Bit adjusts the rearview mirror, a faint light strikes the spirit of Uncle Peck, who is sitting in the back seat of the car. She sees him in the mirror. She smiles at him, and he nods at her. They are happy to be going for a long drive together. Li'l Bit slips the car into first gear; to the audience:)* And then—I floor it. *(Sound of a car taking off. Blackout)*

End of Play

THE MINEOLA TWINS

**A COMEDY IN SIX SCENES,
FOUR DREAMS
AND SIX WIGS**

This play is dedicated to Anne Fausto Sterling.

This play was made possible by generous support from The National Theatre Artist Residency Program administered by Theatre Communications Group and funded by The Pew Charitable Trusts. It was written and developed at the Perseverance Theatre, Douglas, Alaska; Molly D. Smith, Artistic Director.

The Mineola Twins was developed at New York Theatre Workshop in readings and workshops during 1995. The play received its world premiere in November 1996 at Perseverance Theatre in Douglas, Alaska (Molly D. Smith, Artistic Director). Scenic and lighting design was by Arthur Rotch, costumes by Katie Jensen and sound by Dian Martin. Molly D. Smith directed the following cast:

Myra/Myrna	Luan Schooler
Jim/Sarah	Marta Ann Lastufka
Kenny/Ben	Jason Blackwell
Psychiatric Aides/FBI Agents	Mel Sandvik, John Lawson

The Mineola Twins was produced in March 1997 at Trinity Repertory Company, Providence, Rhode Island (Oskar Eustis, Artistic Director; Patricia Egan, Managing Director). Scenic design was by Judy Gailen, costumes by William Lane, lights by Christien Methot and sound by Andrew Keister. Molly D. Smith directed the following cast:

Myra/Myrna	Anne Scurria
Jim/Sarah	Phyllis Kay
Kenny/Ben	Dan Welch
Psychiatric Aides/FBI Agents	Algernon D'Ammassa, Mauro Hantman
Announcer	Amanda Dehnert

THE CHARACTERS

Myrna The "good" twin. Stacked.

Myra The "evil" twin. Played by the same actress as Myrna. Identical to Myrna, except in the chestal area.

Jim Myrna's fiancé.

Kenny Myrna's son.

Ben Myra's son. Played by the same actor as Kenny.

Sarah May be played by an actress who also plays Jim.

Two psychiatric aides, federal agents, etc. Nonspeaking characters who can also help change the furniture.

With the single exception of Sarah, all the characters should be played in a constant state of high hormonal excitement.

TIME

Scenes One and Two take place during the Eisenhower administration.
Scenes Three and Four take place at the beginning of the Nixon administration.
Scenes Five and Six take place during the Bush administration.

There are two ways to do this play:

1. **With good wigs.**
2. **With bad wigs.**

Personally, I prefer the second way.

It would be nice to score this production with female vocalists of the period—Teresa Brewer, Doris Day, Vikki Carr, Nancy Sinatra, etc. These singers were on the Top Ten; as a country, we should never be allowed to forget this.

ABOUT THE VOICE

Words in the script which appear in **boldface** are spoken by the voice that the sisters hear in their dreams. Sometimes The Voice is narrating the sisters' dreams. Sometimes The Voice is prompting the sisters, and sometimes it is The Voice that the sisters have heard in their dreams the night before.

In all these situations, The Voice should be the amplified prerecorded version of the actor who plays Myra and Myrna. At times, the director may choose within a scene to have Myra or Myrna speak in tandem with The Voice.

The result should be a sound impossible to ignore or resist, just like the voice that used to come over the intercom in homeroom. Either brainwashing or subliminal seduction, this voice is the way the sisters talk to each other. In dreams.

Dream Sequence Number One

Eerie lighting. Myra Richards, age seventeen, stands in a trance, in a letter-sweater with several M's stitched on askew; it looks like bloody hands have clutched and stretched the knit during an apocalyptic Sock Hop that ended in disaster. Spooky 1950s sci-fi movie music. The Voice comments to us:

Dream Sequence Number One.
Myra in Homeroom. Myra in Hell.

(A flash of lightning. A crackle of thunder.)

MYRA

So. It was like homeroom, only we were calculating the hypotenuse of hygiene. I whispered to Billy Bonnell, "What does that mean?" And he said, "Yuck-yuck—it's the same angle as the triangle under your skirt, Myra Richards. Yuck-yuck."

"Shut-Up Creep!" Thhwwack! My metal straightedge took off the top of his cranium.

And then Mrs. Hopkins said, in this voice from the crypt, "Miss Richards—what is the hypotenuse of hygiene?"

And just as I was saying, "Excuse Me, Mrs. Hopkins, But I Didn't Know What the Homework Was for Today on Account of Being Suspended Last Week By You 'Cause of the Dumb-Ass Dress Code—"

The Voice cuts in on the intercom:

". . . Get . . . To . . . The . . . Door . . . Now. "

And we all got real scared. And the Nuclear Air-Raid Siren Came On, Real Loud. And kids started bawling and scrambling under their desks. Somehow we knew it was For Real.

We could hear this weird whistling of the bombs coming for us, with a straight line drawn from Moscow to Mineola. Dead Center for the Nassau County Courthouse. Dead Center for Roosevelt Field. And Dead Center for Mineola High. Home of the Mineola Mustangs.

And I knew it would do diddly-squat to get under the desk. Something drew me into the hall, where there was pulsing Red Light and Green Smoke.

Like Christmas in Hell.

I just kept walking.

Kids' bodies were mangled everywhere. Our principal, Mr. Chotner, was hypotenusing under Miss Dorothy Comby's skirt, in the middle of the hall. And the kids in Detention Hall were watching.

I just kept walking.

The Girls' Glee Club had spread-eagled Mr. Koch, the driver's ed. instructor, further down the hall, and they were getting the long-handled custodian's broom out of the closet.

I just kept walking.

I checked my watch. Five minutes to the Apocalypse. I could hear the bombs humming louder now. I thought of crossing against the lights and getting home. But there's nothing lonelier than watching your parents hug while you curl up on the rug alone, and Mom's ceramic dogs melt on the mantel as the sky glows its final Big Red.

Then I heard **The Voice** on the intercom say to me:

"...Find...Her..."

I had to Obey The Voice.

I knew that at the bottom of the stairwell, I would find my twin sister Myrna, hiding from me. Curled up in a little O, her back to me. Just like Old Times in the Womb. A Little O trying to float away from me.

(The Voice begins to breathe rapidly into the microphone)

I entered the stairwell at the top. The lights were out. The air was thick. The stairs were steep. And I heard her soft breathing, trying not to breathe.

She could hear me breathe.
Her soft throat, trying not to swallow.
(The amplified sound of The Voice gulping)
She could taste my saliva.
Her heart, trying not to beat.
(The amplified sound of a beating heart)
She could hear my heart thunder.
(The heart beats faster)
She knew I was there.
And I said:

"I'm Coming, Myrna.
"I'm Coming . . . to Find . . . You . . ."

(A song like Teresa Brewer's "A Sweet Old Fashioned Girl"
plays into the next scene.)

SCENE ONE

1950s

Myrna Richards, age seventeen, is in the midst of closing up the local luncheonette, early evening. Jim Tracy, age twenty-two, in neat attire, prepares to smoke a pipe while waiting for Myrna.

As the scene begins, Myrna is waving good-bye to a customer who has left.

MYRNA

'Night, Mr. Hawkins! Thanks for the tip! Yes, you're right, a dime certainly doesn't go as far as it did—*(Myrna spies Mr. Hawkins's cane, still perched on the counter by his stool)* —Wait! Mr. Hawkins! Your cane!

(Myrna turns toward us and we see her high school clothes are protected by a demure apron. She quickly retrieves the cane, exits offstage, and returns to the doorway) —You're welcome! That's right! Now you can go home and "thwack" Mrs. Hawkins with it! Ha-ha! Good night, now!

(Myrna closes the door to the luncheonette, and flips the closed sign toward the street)

Such a nice man.

(Myrna wipes the counter, straightens chairs. Jim succeeds in lighting his pipe. Myrna sniffs the air in alarm) Did I turn off the grill? I smell something burning—*(Myrna turns and sees Jim smoking his pipe)* Oh, Goodness, Jim!

JIM

Do you like it? I got it today!

MYRNA

Golly! Now I'm engaged to a man who smokes a pipe!

JIM

Well, there we were in the office, puffing cigarettes in the marketing session, trying to come up with ideas for this new car that Ford is designing. And that's when it hit me. I thought: That's it! A pipe!

MYRNA

Very dashing.

JIM

(Suddenly anxious) But I don't look . . . "intellectual," do I?

MYRNA

Oh no. Not at all.

JIM

Because I don't want to go back to the mailroom. I don't want to stand out too much.

MYRNA

Oh you don't. That's why I fell so hard for you—the way you just blend in.

JIM

Maybe this wasn't such a good idea. After all, Arthur Miller smokes a pipe. . . .

MYRNA

Isn't he the baseball player?

JIM

Darling. That's Joe DiMaggio.

MYRNA

Oh well, you know how I am with names in the newspaper. . . . Arthur Miller, Joe DiMaggio, Joseph Stalin—you're my window on the world.

(Jim puffs importantly.)

JIM

So what's wrong, kitten? I thought we'd agreed not to see each other on school nights.

MYRNA

Oh I know. But I'm so upset, Jim, and I don't know where else to turn—

(Jim takes Myrna in his arms.)

JIM

Tell Big Jim.

MYRNA

(Breaking away) Oh it's that sister of mine again! I swear, the Devil rocked her cradle when Mom was out of the room!

JIM

Oh now, Myra's a little wild, that's all. She lacks your "maturity," but she's not a bad kid—

MYRNA

—There's such meanness in her! I'd swear someone dumped her on our doorstep if it wasn't that we're identical twins—

JIM

—Almost identical. Besides, everyone fights with their siblings—

MYRNA

—I've tried. I really have. We decided, fair and square, to divide the room into equal halves. . . . I drew an imaginary line down the middle, and I said to Myra, reasonably, that she was not to cross that line. Except in the cast of fire or nuclear emergencies.

JIM

That sounds sensible.

MYRNA

If she wants to live in squalor and chaos and *utter filth*, that's fine, that's fine, just do in on *her half*. Except. Except! She discards her dirty socks on my side of the room. How does she get those socks so *dirty*?

JIM

When we get married, you won't have to put up with her dirty socks anymore—you'll only have to put up with mine—

MYRNA

—No, Jim, it's gotten really, really bad. Mom and Daddy had a big blow up with Myra. She's been sneaking out of the house, late at night, to go downtown and God Knows Where Else with those boys she hangs out with—maybe even *Greenwich Village*—

JIM

Well, Greenwich Village isn't exactly Sodom and Gomorrah—

MYRNA

I don't know, Jim. There are an awful lot of girls wearing *pants* down there. *(Very slight shudder)*

Anyway, there's been a horrible, horrible fight. Daddy found out that . . . that Myra's gotten a job in a roadside tavern of ill repute—as a so-called "cocktail waitress!"

JIM

What was your father doing in a house of ill repute?

MYRNA

He said he was having car trouble, and went into the Tic Tock to use the phone—and saw Myra in a skimpy outfit waiting on *men his own age*!

JIM

Well, I'm sure she'll make good wages in tips—

MYRNA

Jim! Mineola is a small but decent town! We can't let Myra ruin our good name!

JIM

Well, why doesn't your father go talk to her?

MYRNA

Oh, you know Daddy. He's a man who doesn't show his feelings. Or speak, for that matter. He's so sweet and tired when he comes home. He just sits in his rocking chair, thumping the arms of his chair. But I can tell he's upset. He's rocking much faster, and thumping and thumping away like his heart is breaking. He even talked at the dinner table last night. He called Myra a Whore of Babylon. But I know he doesn't mean it. He's never even *been* to Babylon.

JIM

Then why don't you have a heart-to-heart between two sisters?

MYRNA

I really wish we could be closer . . . but she . . . scares me.

JIM

She scares you!

MYRNA

No, really, Jim—there's something . . . evil in her. I get scared when . . . I look into her eyes. And then I have the most awful *nightmares*: I dream I'm in homeroom when the air-raid siren comes on and even though it's the end of the civilized world as we know it, Myra tracks me down and . . . and . . . I can't remember. And then I wake up.

JIM

I see. I suppose you want me to talk to her.

MYRNA

Oh Jim, would you? **. . . Find Her.** She's got to quit that job.
I know she'd listen to you. I don't think I can hold up my head
in this town anymore. And I've been trying so hard for the
Homemakers of America Senior Award.

JIM

Honey, people don't mistake you for your sister. You're two
separate people.

MYRNA

It's gotten really bad. This past Sunday, I was conducting class
for the Catholic Youth Organization, and I saw Davy Fowler
passing a note to Billy Dicktel—so I confiscated it. And read
it. And were my cheeks red!

JIM

What did the note say?

MYRNA

It's hard for me to say. Don't look at me. It said . . . it said, . . .
"What does Myra Richards say . . . after . . . she . . . "has sex?"
(Myrna blushes bright red)

JIM	**MYRNA**
"Are all you guys on the same team?"	"Are all you guys on the same team?"

(Jim starts to laugh, and stops.)

JIM

Sorry. I heard that joke in the mailroom at work. Okay,
princess. Let me see that pretty little smile of yours, and I'll
drop in on the Tic Tock tonight, okay?
  (Myrna comes into his arms and puts on her bravest smile)
That's my girl!

MYRNA

But you won't "tarry" in the Tic Tock, will you, Jim? Because if you do—

"I'm Coming To Find You."

(*Jim stares a moment at Myrna; she lightens her tone*) Because sometimes I worry—what if all the other girls find out about my special older man and try to steal him from me?

JIM

What if the football captain happens to glance your way?

MYRNA

The football captain?
(*Myrna's face falls*) I think . . . he's already scored a touchdown at my sister's goalpost.

JIM

Whoops . . . What about the captain of the wrestling team?

MYRNA

Myra was pinned on the mat in round one!

JIM

Track?

MYRNA

Myra's Three-Minute Mile?!

JIM

Golf Team?

MYRNA

Myra's Hole-in—

JIM

—Okay. What if . . . the captain of the Chess Team looks your way?

MYRNA

He's out of luck. I know what I want. It's going to be so grand. In just another year, I'll be out of high school, and I've saved my pennies from waiting tables to take courses from Katherine Gibbs—

JIM

—Except I don't want my wife to work!

MYRNA

Oh I won't for long! Just long enough for us to save a down payment on a little two-bedroom Levittown home.

JIM

If everything goes well with this new ad campaign for Ford— you won't have to work. The bonuses will be pouring in!

MYRNA

Oh. My. That sounds exciting.

(Myrna gets flushed. They start to make out.)

JIM

I'm pledged to secrecy—but you've never seen anything like this car! When it hits, it's going to hit big! The firm's even hiring this poetess to come up with lyrical names—like Fiesta or Bronco or Ford Epiphany! —And wait till you see the grille on this baby—well, I helped a little to come up with the design—it looks just like . . . like— *(Jim gets flushed)* —Well, I can't say. Guys are gonna go crazy over this buggy! Honey, the future is ours! You can stay home and cook to your heart's content! You won't have to go to Katherine Gibbs!

MYRNA

Well, a girl should always be prepared for the future. Once I've learned stenography and typing—when my rising young executive-husband comes home with work from the office— he can put his feet up on the hassock while I Take Dictation.

We'll have a son, and by the time he's three or four, we can afford a three-bedroom house in Great Neck with an office downstairs. Then we'll have a dog, and maybe a daughter, too—

JIM

—Kitten. Maybe we should let some things be a surprise—

(Appropriate music, like Doris Day's "I'll See You in My Dreams" starts to play from the jukebox.)

MYRNA

Oh, I know what kind of surprises you want. Just like a man. You've been spending time reading Mr. Hefner again, haven't you?

JIM

I'm a lonely man on school nights.

MYRNA

Oh Jim. I know. I miss you too on school nights. *(They begin to make out seriously now)* I . . . I just . . . count . . . the minutes until . . . Friday night.

JIM

MMmmm. Me Too. I can't keep my mind on work. *(Jim shifts Myrna's weight against him)*

MYRNA

You . . . you don't mind, do you, Jim? Waiting for me?

JIM

It's . . . hard. Awfully . . . hard. Myrna— *(Jim has started to loosen Myrna's items of clothing)*

MYRNA

Oh . . . Jim. Jim . . . *(Myrna starts to help him)* —Wait—I'm getting choked a little—there. That's better.

JIM

You've put the "closed sign" up, didn't you?

MYRNA

We're locked up . . . "tight."

JIM

Quick . . . turn off the overhead lights—

(Myrna complies. She comes back, panting slightly.)

MYRNA

My. This *is* a treat for a school night.
   (Jim lifts Myrna up on a stool. She wraps herself around him. Suddenly, Myrna stops, puzzled) Jim. How come, if Myra and I are identical twins, that we're not . . . identical? I mean, how come she's . . .

JIM

Flat as a pancake?

MYRNA

(Giggling) True. And I'm so . . .

JIM

Stacked, darling. Like a stack of pancakes.

MYRNA

Yes. But I mean, is it scientifically possible? Wouldn't either both of us be . . . you know— *(Myrna runs her hands coquettishly over her breasts)*

JIM

Yes, yes— *(Jim starts unsnapping Myrna's brassiere beneath her blouse)*

MYRNA

—Or we'd both be like Iowa in the chestal region?

(Jim now helps Myrna step out of her underwear beneath her skirt.)

JIM

You're just lucky, I guess. I'm . . . just lucky. Please, God, let me be lucky tonight— *(Jim nibbles on Myrna's neck. She moans)*

MYRNA

Bloodlines . . . science and all that . . . it's just . . . so . . . strange.

JIM

Let's not talk about your sister anymore tonight. Let's not talk.

(Jim presses against Myrna; throughout the following the petting gets hotter until Myrna clambers up on all fours onto two adjoining stools and Jim gets on his knees on the adjacent stool.)

MYRNA

Oh! Oh Jim! Oh . . . Oh Jim!

JIM

Myrna . . .

MYRNA

Jim, Jim, Jim—

JIM

(Urgently) Myrna, Myrna—

MYRNA

—Yes! Right now! Jim! Now! Now! Ohhh—Jimbo-ooohhh— WAIT! *(Jim, red-faced and behind Myrna, stops stock-still)* Jim—this—this isn't right.

JIM

Oh, Myrna—

MYRNA

These stools are giving me motion sickness. *(Myrna climbs down with iron will)* We . . . we shouldn't be doing this.

(Myrna looks behind and sees Jim rotating on his stool in frustration. She stops him from spinning) Darling—I want you. Badly. But not now. Not here. I want it to be so . . . right. Not with the smell of meatloaf still in the air. And it will . . . it will be . . . so "right," won't it? Jim?

JIM

I guess.

(Jim and Myrna do not speak to each other for a beat. They adjust their clothing. Myrna picks up her undies with great dignity, tucking the cotton into her apron pockets.)

MYRNA

I want to be pure for you on our Wedding Day.

JIM

Oh, Myrna . . . You are pure. You have been pure. You will always be pure.

MYRNA

No, Jim—Virginity is a state of mind.

JIM

But, Myrna, Baby—

MYRNA

No Buts. You can't be more or less a Virgin. It's different for men. There are no absolutes for guys. I have to earn the right to wear white when I walk down the aisle.

(Jim sighs wearily.)

MYRNA

Oh my. I haven't filled the sugar and condiment bottles yet.

(There is an awkward pause as Jim finds his pipe and knocks out the ashes)
Please, darling. Tell me you understand.

(Jim's Adam's apple bobs as he speaks.)

JIM

I understand, Myrna. You're a good girl. It's just that God built Men with this . . . "design flaw." It's not great for an automotive body much less the engine to torque it up like that without letting the throttle go. Do you understand what I'm talking about?

MYRNA

(Confused) Automobiles?

JIM

No. I'm talking about . . . agony.

(Myrna, concerned, turns to Jim to hold him.)

MYRNA

Oh Jim. I'm so sorry.

JIM

Don't *touch* me. Not right now. I've got to . . . let the engine cool down.

MYRNA

Oh Jim. I don't understand about these things. But if there was . . . something . . . something I could do without compromising my innocence . . . something that . . . might make you feel better—would you tell me?

(Jim thinks a moment, tempted. Then his better angel decides.)

JIM

Maybe I'd better go. It's getting late.

(Jim takes a huge breath) There. It's not . . . "hurting" as much now. I think I can walk.

MYRNA

Jim!

JIM

You are so . . . good. You're the only absolute goodness in my life. Let's say good night while we have no regrets.

MYRNA

You're my guiding light, Jim. Will I see you Friday night?

(Jim half-hobbles, half-sidles in a strange crab-walk to the luncheonette door.)

JIM

You bet.
    (He manages a half-smile from the doorway) I'd better find that sister of yours and give her a talking to.

(Jim exits. Myrna flies to the door, and waves angelically at his retreating figure.)

MYRNA

Good night, darling! . . . Till Friday!
    (Myrna turns, worry now on her face. In a whisper, she addresses the Deity in the hush of the luncheonette:) Please, God, Please—let Jim wait for me!

(Fifties music swells as the lights dim into Scene Two.)

SCENE TWO

Later That Evening

We see the interior of a cheap motel used for trysts of G.I.'s on leave from Mitchell Air Force Base. The blinking neon of "MOTEL" flashes throughout the scene.

At the start of the scene, Myra sits up in bed, agitated. She wears a push-up Maidenform bra and a panty-girdle. Myra manages to smoke furiously while cracking her gum.

There is a heap in the bed beside her, curled under the cheap chintz spread, completely covered, and hogging the entire bedspread. Occasionally, we hear muffled sobs.

MYRA

"I like Ike. I Like Ike." I mean, is that cornball or what? Can you believe how way-in this country is? They voted for that square twice!

(Myra stops, pops her gum. Listens to the heap) Hey, man. Hey, daddy. I'm trying, see? I'm trying to "engage," dig? I'm dishing politics, man, I'm trying to connect.

(Myra nudges the heap) Hey. Hey. You gonna come out sometime this decade?

(The heap covers itself with some insistence) Hey. Suit yourself, daddy-O. No skin offa my pearlie-whites. I've had cats cry before the Act, and I've had lottsa cats wail during. You're the first one to boo-hoo after.

(Myra tries again) Hey, I gotta idea. You got any bread? Any wheels? We could just spook in your bomb and get some burgers. Or we could peel on outta here and spin into the Village. It's crazy down there, any night of the week. We go take in the Vanguard—do you dig that scene? It's the most,

the meanest . . . we could do a set, then blow the joint and just walk around the streets.

There's this one guy, Ace, who walks around with a *parrot* on his shoulder. It's crazy. He's so hip—you pay him a dime, and he gives you a poem on the spot. He poetizes on a dime. And these poems—they don't rhyme or anything. They're deep. They don't *mean*, they just *are*. It's far-out!

(Jim, in a fury, pops up.)

JIM

Speak English, can't you! If you want to talk to me, speak English! English!

MYRA

Wow.

(Jim huddles, still clutching the spread around him.)

JIM

Jesus. You've watched too many James Dean movies.

(Myra chokes up at the mention of James Dean.)

MYRA

He only made *three*. And then he *died*.

JIM

Hey, look, I wasn't making fun of him or anything.

MYRA

He was important to a lot of people. He lived fast, died young . . . and really messed up his face.

JIM

I'm sure he was important to impressionable young women. But that doesn't mean he could act. Couldn't drive, either.

MYRA

Oh, he could drive. It was the yo-yo on the other side of the yellow line he didn't count on. I'll bet he was going over a hundred in that Spyder, the top down, he was flying, he was putting something down! Some asshole yo-yo in a *Ford*, for God's sake.

(Jim clears his throat.)

JIM

The Ford Motor Company happens to be one of my clients.

MYRA

Oh. That's nice. What do you do for them?

JIM

Well, I advise them on strategies for younger buyers under twenty-five. We're devising a new model that's going to sweep aside the competition.

MYRA

So where is this company of yours where you work at devising and sweeping?

JIM

Madison Avenue.

MYRA

You work in Manhattan? And you don't live there?

JIM

I like more air and more space and more *green*.

MYRA

Oh man. You're free, white, over twenty-one, and you get to get up every morning and take the LI—double—R into Manhattan. If I were you, I'd cash in the return ticket to Mineola and find a pad like *(Snap)* that.

JIM

You'll get your chance.

MYRA

Not soon enough. You think if you get a wife and one of those cornball aprons and tongs and barbecue hamburgers in Mineola on the weekends, your bosses will promote you faster?

JIM

There's nothing wrong with Mineola.

MYRA

(Exploding) What is there to do in Mineola? Go to bingo, go to the PTA, fight over whether or not *Catcher in the Rye* should be allowed in our libraries! Mineola's so dull, there wasn't even a Red Scare here! In Mineola, people keep their blinds up because *nothing happens* on a Saturday night.

JIM

You are full of hate.

MYRA

I'm restless! Don't you sometimes feel like you're gonna jump out of your skin if you don't do something, go somewhere?

JIM

Well, sometimes.

MYRA

Yeah? And then what do you do?

JIM

I go for a nice, brisk walk around the block.

MYRA

How old are you?

JIM

(In his deepest chest voice) I'm . . . twenty-two. Going on twenty-three.

MYRA

Oh man. I've done it with juvenile delinquents older than you.

JIM

I'll bet you have.
        (Pause. They shift in the bed)
        So—this fellow with the parrot—Ace?

MYRA

Yeah, Ace.

JIM

What is his poetry like?

MYRA

It's hard to describe in words. It's like jazz riffs without the music. It's just a torrent of feeling and colors and *truth*.

JIM

No rhyme?

MYRA

Rhyme is out. Square. Dead.

JIM

Look, I've read *On the Road*.

MYRA

You have?

JIM

Yes. In hardcover.

MYRA

Jeez. I've never done it with anyone else who's read Kerouac.

(This pleases Jim.)

JIM

So I'm your first?

MYRA

In that way, you are. Nobody reads Kerouac in Mineola. So. What did you think?

JIM

Of Kerouac? It was kind of long.

MYRA

Yeah. Dull. *(They smile at this small island of agreement)* You're okay for a man who wears ties.

JIM

You're okay, too. You're nothing like your sister— *(It strikes Jim)* —Oh my God! Your sister! Oh, God, Oh God—

MYRA

Look don't clutch on me, Jim. . . . Hang Loose, okay? Just breathe. It's gonna be all right.

JIM

Oh, man, what am I going to tell her?

MYRA

We'll keep it a secret from little Miss Tom Peep.

JIM

Oh, God. She'll look into my eyes. She'll know.

MYRA

What, you think your eyes are gonna look different now? Oh, boy, where did you get your information? Health classes at Mineola High? Although I bet you are going to walk in a different way. You know what they call it when they lower the front end of a car to streamline it? So it's real fast for drag-ging? They call it "raking." And that's you, daddy-O. You've been raked.

JIM

I've got to think. You've got to help me think.
   (Myra snaps her gum) Could you maybe not pop your gum?

(Myra, with great ceremony, removes her gum and places it on the headboard.)

MYRA

Okay, now we can think great thoughts. Okay. You don't tell her, she doesn't ask. Don't ask, don't tell. The formula for mod-ern marriages.

JIM

You sound like an expert. When are you getting married?

MYRA

Hardehar-har. There's never been a movie made that's even close to how I'm gonna live. I'm making it up from scratch. No marriage. No children. No suburbs. Just freedom!

JIM

But you're a girl! You can't do that!

MYRA

I am going to spend my life doing everything people tell me I can't do.

(Beat.)

JIM

Maybe I should think over this marriage thing.

MYRA

Look, Jim—you gotta marry my sister. She's been collecting recipes until she has dinner completely planned for the first year.

JIM

Are you hot? There's no air in here—

MYRA

And she's been practicing her signature, "Mrs. James Tracy. Mrs. James Tracy. Mrs. James Tracy."

JIM

I'm seeing things differently now. I've been "raked."

MYRA

Oh shit. She's gonna blame me.

JIM

No, see, Myrna was right. It's the domino-theory. Let's say nobody notices anything different about me, right? I look the same, talk the same, almost walk the same. Tomorrow morning, I go into work, nobody notices. A year from now, I walk down the aisle with my intended, your sister, and she doesn't know the difference.

MYRA

I'm with you so far.

JIM

So Virginity *is* a state of mind. It's a figment of the imagination.

MYRA

That's what I was trying to say a while back when you were boo-hooing.

JIM

So don't you see? The domino-theory? There goes virginity, there goes my promotion, my work ethic, monogamy, mortgages, raising 2.5 children, truth in advertising, belief in a deity, living in the suburbs, caring for my aged parents and saluting the flag.

MYRA

Wow. Heavy. *(Jim and Myra sit next to each other in bed. They contemplate)*
     Wanna cigarette? *(Myra offers her pack)*

JIM

Sure.

(They puff.)

MYRA

My brain hurts. That usually never happens *after* sex.

JIM

Yeah. I guess.

MYRA

So this was your first time.

JIM

Yes. . . . Myra? Was I—could you tell me—was I—

MYRA

You were wonderful, Jimmy. You know, I've never known anyone like you, Jim Tracy. You're the kind of guy a girl could dream about.

JIM

Thanks. . . . Myra? How "many" guys have you—

MYRA

Gone all the way with? To Home Plate?

JIM

Yes. Do you mind my asking?

MYRA

Well, there are all the guys on the first string—and I'm working on the second string who have their letters—

JIM

Whoa! So it's really true about you. You really are the Whore of Babylon!

MYRA

Hey! Wait a minute! First of all, I happen to really like football. Second of all, we just jammed on a philosophical thing here, like a neutrality of moral consequence, so where do you get off calling me that? Putting that down?

JIM

I was talking about me. Men are defined by what they do—their actions in the world. It's different for you—you're a girl. There are . . . absolutes in the world for girls. Girls don't do, they just are.

(Furious, Myra gets out of bed and starts dressing. She tries not to cry.)

MYRA

Why—why did you have to do this? I thought . . . for a minute—I thought you were different. I thought you understood.

JIM

Why are you getting all steamed up? I'm just another "notch" on your belt, right?—

MYRA

—I hope my next decade is better than this one.

JIM

I mean, girls are born the way they are. Men *become.*

MYRA

I can't believe I fall for it every time.

JIM

Myrna was born "good." You were born . . . "nice."

MYRA

I'm cool to the guys, thinking, dip that I am, that they're gonna be cool back. I don't get it, I really don't. I'm nice to you, right? I made you feel good, I felt good, we both felt good together, no questions asked, no demands—why then do you guys always do this?

JIM

So the bottom line is—you did sleep with the football team.

(Myra reaches the door, disheveled but dressed. She turns, goes back for her gum on the headboard.)

MYRA

Well, lucky for us one of us had some experience.

(Myra puts the gum in her mouth. Just then, there is a timid tapping on the motel room door. Myra and Jim freeze.)

MYRNA

(Offstage; sobbing) Jim? Jim? . . . Jiiimm?

MYRA

(Hissed) Shit!

JIM

(Feverishly whispered) O migod . . . o migod . . . omigod—

MYRA

Is this like the goddamn Alamo? Or is there a backdoor?

(Jim puts his trousers on backwards; Myra checks out the bathroom.)

MYRNA

(Off) Oh, Jim—I know you're in there. I know, Jim. You're in there with— (Sob) —HER.

(There is a continued sobbing and tapping on the door.)

MYRA

(Stage whisper) There's a window over the toilet—it's gonna be a tight squeeze—lucky for me I don't have any tits. Give me the keys to your car.

(Sob, tap on the door. Jim is in a state of shock. Myra grabs him) Your car. Your car, daddy-O. Give Me the Goddamn Keys. Now.

(Jim reaches into his trouser pockets awkwardly; she grabs the keys out of his shaking hands)

Kiss Her Good Night for me. I'm outta here.

(Myra rushes into the bathroom. We hear a window being pried open, a faint "oooff" of pain, and a thud. Meanwhile on the front door, the wounded thrush tapping has changed into the staccato pounding of a killer.)

MYRNA

(Off) MYRA! I'M GONNA KILL YOU, MYRA! WAIT TILL I GET MY HANDS AROUND YOUR SCRAWNY LITTLE NECK! MYRA! YOU SUCK, MYRA! I'M GONNA RIP OFF WHAT LITTLE THERE IS OF YOUR KNOCKERS, MYRA! I'M GONNA USE YOUR ITSIES FOR MY KEY CHAIN, MYRA! I WILL NEVER TALK TO YOU AGAIN! *OPEN* (Pound) THIS (Pound) DOOR! (Pound)

(A huge thump. A beat. Then, the wounded thrush tactic again. The sound of a tremulous little girl writhing against the door in agony, who wouldn't hurt a fly, but might slash her wrists)

(Little butterfly sobs of pathos; off) J-jiimm? Baby? Jjiimm-bo? Honey—I know it isn't your fault. I know how good you are . . . baby—just let me in, let me see you, Jim . . . don't send me away. . . . Jimm? Jimmy? Jimmy-Jim?

(Jim, moved by her pleas, scared, catatonic, sidles to the door with his backwards trousers falling down. He tentatively unlocks the door.)

JIM

(Sobbing) Myrna? Baby? There's—there's no one here—

(As Myrna hears the door lock click, she throws herself into the room with a Medea-scream:)

MYRNA

I'LL KILL YOU!!!

(Jim lands on his butt. Myrna flies across the room. They blink at each other in the disheveled room. As Myrna picks up something from the floor, there is the sound of Jim's automobile being quickly started, revved, and thrown into reverse outside the room) Shhh—ootttt!

(Myrna runs to the door, too late. She watches a car offstage screech out of the parking lot into the night. Her shoulders slump. Jim huddles where he is. A beat. Myrna turns, limp and tired, with a single dirty sock that Myra has cast-off dangling from her hand in silent accusation. They both stare at the sock. Blackout.)

SCENE THREE

1969

We see Myrna, muffled in a trench coat, a head scarf and dark glasses, standing in line for a teller at the Roosevelt Savings and Loan in downtown Mineola. She is visibly paranoid, checking around her while trying to remain discrete. Myrna has hardened slightly, small lines of discontent forming around her mouth. She is a woman who continues to embrace the fifties; only the hem of her skirt tells us it is actually 1969.

Beside her is her son Kenny, a slight, sensitive teenager, dressed in a paisley shirt and blue bell-bottom denims with a button fly. Kenny is listening to a brand-new transistor radio.

KENNY

They're still hunting! She's the last one of the gang still on the loose! That guy who was the leader was killed in a shoot-out upstate! Whoa! But there's no sign of her!

MYRNA

If you're not going to listen to Casey Kasem, young man, you are to turn your radio off. *Now.*

(A beat. They move up in the line) What happened to that poor guard?

KENNY

Still in the hospital.

MYRNA

I can't believe a member of my immediate family attacked someone in uniform. They are going to nail her hiney.

KENNY

Only if they catch her.

MYRNA

If there's any justice in this world, Aunt Myra will be making license plates the rest of her life. That should help put an end to the War in Vietnam. Instead of shacking up with radicals and the SDS, she'll have to fend off hefty female inmates in the shower when she drops her soap!

KENNY

Mom!

MYRNA

Well, for heaven's sake, Kenny, I know she's family, but she should use common sense! How does— *(Myrna lowers her voice)* —how does holding up the Roosevelt Savings and Loan in downtown Mineola help in ending the war!

KENNY

All I know is this is the most exciting thing to happen on Long Island Ever! Usually when I walk in the cafeteria, the guys from industrial ed try to tear off the fruit loop on the back of my shirt! Now when I walk into the lunch room, kids give me their desserts! They think Aunt Myra's cool!

(Beat. They wait in the bank line.)

MYRNA

I *hate* coming to this bank. *(Pause)* Is anyone looking at us?

KENNY

No. We're ordinary.

MYRNA

What really gripes my ass is I'm now a prisoner in my own house! I moved us to a nice neighborhood in Great Neck; I volunteered for the Nixon for President Campaign. I leafleted

downtown for harsh control of subversives. And now gentlemen who look like Mormon Missionaries are parked outside
my door in unmarked white Fords drinking coffee in styrofoam cups!

(The two move up in line) When your Aunt Myra held up
this bank, knowing darn well your grandmother and my joint
savings is in here, she deliberately padded her brassiere so she
could pass as me! My sister used my knockers as terrorist
camouflage!

KENNY

Mom!

*(Just then, two men who look like Mormon missionaries in
trench coats holding styrofoam cups enter and stand casually
by a counter.)*

KENNY

I think they're here.

MYRNA

My taxes are paying for this. *(Beat)* It would have been nice,
son, if you hadn't changed out of your nice school clothes that
I just bought for you.

(Pause. Myrna and Kenny move up in line.)

KENNY

It's bad enough that I have to dress like a Hitler Youth all day
in school because of our Nazi principal and his Nazi dress
code.

MYRNA

Kenny! Lower your voice. No one wants to hear your counter-
cultural nonsense.

KENNY

It's the *Truth*.

MYRNA

You Make Me Laugh. If it wasn't for your grandfather and other men like him who fought for your freedom, you'd be singing "Deutschland Über Alles" every morning in home room. —Nazis! Hitler Youth!

KENNY

Yeah? What about Mayor Daley's stormtroopers at the Democratic Convention? —

MYRNA

—I do not want to have this discussion with you in public. It is not a good time right now. You could have a little concern for your mother's nerves right now and do your utmost to not attract attention. I wish I could be a teenager again. Everything's an absolute: Good, Evil; Black, White; McCarthy, Nixon. There's no gray. Nothing relative. Just you passing judgment. It must be wonderful to be fourteen and perfect, absolutely in the right, absolutely—

(Myrna suddenly stops and has a strange comatose seizure; we hear the echo of electric shock therapy. Kenny also stops, and watches her in alarm and guilt.)

KENNY

(Whispered) Mom? *(Kenny waits, we hear the electric buzzing start to fade)* Mom? Mom! *(Kenny shakes her. Myrna "comes to")* You went off again.

MYRNA

Sorry.

(Beat.)

KENNY

What happens to you? When you . . . go off . . . like that?

MYRNA

It's nothing to be scared about, Kenny. It's just a residual effect of the . . . the therapy I had.

KENNY

But what's it like? Where do you go?

MYRNA

I go back to a more peaceful time. Back to high school. When I still had a shot at the Homemaker's of America Senior Award. Long before I *was* a homemaker.

KENNY

Do you want to go home?

MYRNA

I'm fine.

KENNY

Is Dad coming home tonight?

(Myrna's mouth tightens slightly.)

MYRNA

No. It will be just the two of us—having a wonderful time: a private date with a very handsome young beau—a few candles, and a new recipe. A special casserole with pineapple fritters!

KENNY

Yes ma'am. . . . Can we have hamburger sometime this week?

MYRNA

You don't like my casseroles.

KENNY

They're . . . different.

MYRNA

Ever since my "medication" and "treatment"—something's happened to all my recipes. Before I went into the hospital, I was a wonderful cook.

KENNY

You're still an okay cook, Mom.

MYRNA

Ask Grandma. She still has all my ribbons and medals from high school. I won every bake-off. Well. Bygone days.

(Jim Tracy, now down on his luck, in shoddy clerical attire, stands in the cashier's cage. Myrna and Kenny are now first in line.)

JIM

Next.

MYRNA

Oh, Lord. Is there another cashier available?

KENNY

Go on, Mom. That man has called you.

MYRNA

Kenny—go to the counter over there and wait for me.

(Kenny complies. He looks at the FBI agents who sip their coffee and look at him. Myrna advances to the cashier cage. Jim tries to be officious, but the exchange breaks into urgent whispering.)

JIM

How may I help you?

MYRNA

I'd like to make a withdrawal from a joint savings account—here. I expect you'll want to verify the signature.

JIM

That's fine. . . . Myrna!

MYRNA

(Stiffly) Please. It's Mrs. O'Brien.

JIM

But you're well?

MYRNA

I'm fine, thank you. I'd appreciate large bills, please.

JIM

Yes, Mrs. O'Brien. —May I tell you how sorry I am about the trouble with your sister?

MYRNA

I think that's in questionable taste.

JIM

Oh for God's sake, Myrna! Can't you just talk to me a little?

MYRNA

Would you please expedite my withdrawal? My son is with me, and I'm in a bit of a hurry—

JIM

—Just look at me, just a little, Myrna—

(Myrna looks at him. Beat.)

MYRNA

When's the last time you bought a proper suit? And a nice tie?

JIM

I know. I—I have . . . nothing.

MYRNA

Is this what you want for yourself? To be a . . . "bank cashier?"

JIM

At least I get to see you once a week. I tried bagging groceries at your A&P, but I wasn't fast enough.

MYRNA

What is it you want from me?

JIM

Couldn't we just have lunch together? Myrna? At our old luncheonette? Just . . . lunch?

MYRNA

I am a *married* woman.

JIM

I know but—do you love your husband?

MYRNA

(A bit loudly) Do I have to call the manager?

(The agents look at them. Myrna and Jim recover their composure, and go back to surreptitious whispering.)

JIM

That will not be necessary. Large bills, I believe you said?

MYRNA

Yes—that's right.
   (Jim counts the money, biting his lip)
Thank you.
   (As Myrna starts to leave) For God's sake, Jim, go back to school, do something with your life, leave Mineola!—

(Jim brightens; Myrna has talked to him. She abruptly leaves.)

JIM

Myrna!

(Myrna joins Kenny at the counter. The agents relax, study the income tax brochures and bank promotional literature.)

MYRNA

I hate coming to this bank.

KENNY

Can we go now?

MYRNA

You know the story of the prodigal son? This man had two sons, right, and one worked hard in the fields from dawn to dusk. He never gave his parents cause to worry. The other son was a real *fuck-up*. I'm sorry, no other word will do. He never saved one thin dime, and he drank whatever money he filched from the family business. The prodigal son got into trouble with the law. He had to hide in this foreign land far across the borders, and a price was on his head. And he thought—Wait a minute, I'll bet I can get Mom sorry for me, and she'll dip into the old man's pockets when he's asleep. And so he came dragging home in clothes that hadn't been washed in weeks. And his aged parents bailed him out. They drew his bathwater. They washed his clothes. And they barbecued up filet mignon. And do you know what the good son felt, when he came home from the fields and saw his evil brother getting the ticker-tape parade? *What am I, ground chuck?*

(Myrna stops. The buzzing is loud. Kenny waits, and then shakes her slightly.)

KENNY

Mom? Mom?

(Myrna "comes to" and continues; the buzzing goes out.)

MYRNA

The Good Brother bided his time, and then went to the cops in the other country and turned his sorry brother in; took the reward, and invested it. And then, in a hostile takeover, he got control of his father's business. He sent his parents to a nice, clean nursing home where they had arts therapy. And when the prodigal son was finally released from the hoosegow, he had to beg in the marketplace, until the Prodigal Son finally *died*. And the Good Son danced and danced. Happy Ending!

KENNY

I don't remember the story like that.

MYRNA

No?

(Myrna takes a breath) Now I want you to listen carefully to me, son. What your Aunt Myra did was wrong. This is our country, love it or leave it. You have to respect our president and our laws. Whether it's registering for the draft or scooping up after your dog.

(Myrna takes another breath) But family is family. Blood is blood. . . . Now listen, Kenny—you are not ever, ever to tell your father what we are about to do—

(Myrna and Kenny turn in the direction of the other counter where the agents are engrossed in their pamplets and balancing their checkbooks. They turn back.)

KENNY

Are we going to help Aunt Myra?

MYRNA

Yes. We are. You are. I'm asking you to be a grown man tonight, son. I can't go myself to help Myra—she only trusts you. I am driving you to Bobby's house, as if you're spending the night. You will ring the bell, go inside and talk to Bobby. I will drive off as a diversion, and the white unmarked Ford will follow me. When you are sure the coast is clear, slip out of Bobby's house by the back door, and walk to the train station. Get the 4:55 to New York. Aunt Myra says you're to get in the last car, and at each station change cars. That way you'll know if you're being followed. When you reach Grand Central Station, take the local IRT downtown to Astor Place. Walk carefully to St. Mark's Place, and then turn right on Second Avenue. Walk two blocks east on East Fifth St., and check if you're being followed. Go into the luncheonette on Fifth and First Avenue, and buy a hamburger and a coke. Eat it slowly. Then retrace your steps to this address— *(Myrna hands Kenny a folded slip of paper)* It's between Second and First. Don't tarry, and don't talk to *anyone*. Especially men with long hair and earrings. Aunt Myra is on the top floor, door to the left. Is this clear?

KENNY

Wow. Cool.

MYRNA

Above all else, do not stay longer than it takes. Do You Understand? Here— *(From a pocket of her coat, Myrna draws out a small fold of bills)* —This is money for your ticket on the Long Island Railroad, your subway, and when you're done with Aunt Myra, you are to walk up to Union Square and hail a cab home to Nassau County. Do not walk around in the Village.

KENNY

What's wrong with the Village? The Village is safe!

MYRNA

Kenny. I'll be worried sick about you.

KENNY

Yes ma'am. . . . This is the most exciting day of my entire life.

(With solemnity, Myrna draws out a bulging envelope from her coat pocket.)

MYRNA

I'm trusting you with a great deal, Kenny. The money inside the envelope is from Grandma. Grandma cashed in a five thousand dollar treasury bond for Myra.

> **KENNY**

Whoa.

> **MYRNA**

To help a criminal. That five thousand dollars should get Myra across the border into Canada and start a new life. When Myra gets to Canada, she's to change her name, change her hair color, and copy *someone else's* face. And she's never to be in touch with us again.

> **KENNY**

Mom, what if Dad gets home before I do?

> **MYRNA**

Okay, Kenny, it's cut the crap time. You and I both know your father's shacked up at the Plaza with his secretary for the rest of the weekend.

> **KENNY**

She's nice. She likes to wear mauve.

(Myrna narrows her eyes with suspicion.)

> **MYRNA**

I don't like hearing the word "mauve" in your mouth. Only boys who grow up to be interior decorators use words like "mauve."

> **KENNY**

Mom!

> **MYRNA**

Maybe it's all that time Myra spent baby-sitting you while I was "indisposed." In the "hospital." Myra was spoon-feeding you mashed banana and Mao Tse-Tung! And teaching you words like "Mauve!"

(The buzzing begins again; Kenny pleads.)

KENNY

Please don't get upset.

(Myrna draws out something white from her coat pocket.)

MYRNA

One last thing—you are to hand your Aunt Myra this.

(Beat.)

KENNY

Why would I give her a dirty sock?

MYRNA

She'll know why. Say that the sock is from me. I've saved it all these many years just for a moment like this. Because many years ago, your Aunt Myra took something precious, someone very dear, and tossed it all away like a used sock.

I want her to transport this dirty sock over the Canadian border. I want her to take her disrespect and her dirty sock with her. And when she misses all the wonderful things America has, she can finger this dirty sock and think about the choices she made.

(Beat)

Meet me out front. I'll go get the car.

(As Myrna exits, the FBI agents hold open the door for her) Thank you, gentlemen. How's your coffee?

(Kenny, left behind for a second with Myra's sock in his hand, regards it with devotion. He feels someone staring at him, turns and sees Jim Tracy at the cashier's window. Kenny stuffs the sock in his pocket and runs after his mother.)

Dream Sequence Number Two

We see Myrna in a hospital johnny. Her hair has not been tended to in some time. Occasionally, there is an electronic buzzing underneath the institutional Muzac which begins to play.

Two psychiatric aides run in slow motion behind Myrna; they catch up and restrain her, one at each elbow. The effect, though, is of a choreographed dance routine, which, in fact, it is. Throughout the following monologue, Myrna spins beyond their reach; caught and lifted by each aide in turn, dipping and twirling. The aides are unable to fasten Myrna into a straitjacket.

The Voice tells us:

Dream Sequence Number Two.
Myrna in the Hospital. Myrna in Hell.

MYRNA

So. I will be dressed in my London Fog raincoat, with my Coach bag accessories, neatly coifed, because Dr. Prior says hygiene is a sign of mental health.

I'll park behind the trailer, next to the dump right off Jericho Turnpike. Then I'll knock at her screen door.

My sister will answer the door, still drowsy from her night shift. But she'll pretend not to be surprised.

"Can I come in?" I'll ask.

She turns and leaves the screen door open.

I enter. It's a pigsty; high heels are dropped willy-nilly; dirty dishes pile in the sink. A trail of socks leads to the platform bed in the back.

She sits down at the table and waits.

"Listen—" I say, "—can we have a cup of tea together?"

As she makes the tea, I chatter. She searches for a clean cup. It's not very. She pours the water. She dumps the cups on the table and the water sloshes over the rim of my cup. You'd swear she was never a waitress. —"Oh Myra—" I say "—you've left the stove on!"

As my sister turns, swiftly I take the vial from my pocket and pour it into her cup. Then I quickly add two sugars and stir as she turns back.

"You do take sugar, don't you?" She does. I don't. I never have.

We sip our tea.

"There's bad blood between us, Myra. **No one could clear up the bad blood."**

Myra nods. Her head continues to nod in slower and slower circles. I catch the teacup before it falls, the drug already coursing through her blood.

Quickly I go to work. I put on my Playtex Living Gloves, my rain bonnet and my London Fog. I carefully wash her cup, and put it away. I put the suicide note on the table with the handwriting that looks just like hers, the letters trailing off after:

"I Can't Go On This Way. . . ."

Then I open the trunk of my car and take out Daddy's Hunting Rifle. I giggle, because I'd never held anything more dangerous than a soup ladle.

But I know just what to do. Kneeling beside my sister, I take off her right shoe. I toss it on the floor. I take off her right sock—I just toss it. Then I brace the rifle at a jaunty angle so that her big toe jams the trigger while her mouth sucks the double barrel—just like old times with the football team.

(Amplified sound of breathing)

Then I kneel beside her and whisper:

"This is real, you asshole, this is happening."

(Amplified sound of The Voice gulping)

For the first time in years, my sister and I touch as I press her big toe on the trigger.

(Amplified sound of a beating heart)

We squeeze the trigger together.

It sounds like *champagne*. I don't want to look. I expect to see hamburger, ground chuck at forty-nine cents a pound. But from the stem of her neck, where her head used to be—there's a bouquet. Her brains have flowered. *Les Fleurs du mal*. "It's so pretty, Myra!" I tell her. I touch a single stem. I'll take a flower home and press it in my diary.

Maybe when he's old enough, I'll give it to Kenny.

Kenny.

What am I going to tell little Kenny?

(The two psychiatric aides finally restrain Myrna in the jacket, but the three continue to dance the choreographed routine, in complete Hollywood harmony)

The truth. Tell Kenny the truth.

(Myrna smiles beatifically at her dance partners/keepers)

Aunt Myra has gone on a long, long trip. Far across the border.

(The smile turns into a grin)

And she's never coming back.

(The electronic buzzing grows as the aides escort Myrna off-stage.)

SCENE FOUR

Later That Evening

Myra sits on a mattress on a floor in an apartment in the East Village. There are political posters on the wall advertising marches, Jimi Hendrix, love, peace, etc. In one corner of the room, there is a bong; in another a lava lamp. There is a single chair. Myra sits cross-legged on the mattress, a roll of toilet paper beside her for kleenex as she weeps. She clutches the dirty sock. Beside her is a can of Coca-Cola. Kenny is lying on the floor on his stomach, his hand holding hers.

MYRA

Kenny. Oh man, Kenny. Shit, Ken.

(Myra weeps into the sock. Kenny takes the sock away and hands Myra the toilet roll.)

KENNY

Use the toilet paper, okay? You don't know where that sock has been.

MYRA

I really really really fucked up.

KENNY

It could be worse.

MYRA

Did they catch Hacker yet?

KENNY

Yeah. He might be dead or something.

MYRA

Oh man. First Malcolm, then Che and now—Hacker. Hacker.
He was a maniac. He was kinda an asshole, too. But he was
a great lover. Out of all the guys on the National Council, he
was the best. *(She sniffles)* Gave me chlamydia, too. That's
what happens when you sleep with the leadership. Well, at
least I'll have a keepsake.

KENNY

What's chlamydia?

MYRA

Oh, shit. You can't stay here. We've got to move.

KENNY

Nobody followed me.

MYRA

You sure?

KENNY

I was real careful.

MYRA

You're my brave, smart nephew. How you can be my sister's
son is one of those mysteries of genetics.

KENNY

Mom's pretty pissed.

MYRA

It's Grandma's money.

KENNY

I know.

MYRA

I'm gonna pay it back. I'm gonna get a good job in Toronto;
no more collectives.

KENNY

I know.

MYRA

I've got to be on my guard. I've got to stay alert.

(Shakily, Myra draws out a pill.)

KENNY

What's that?

MYRA

It's . . . "medicine." Methedrine. It keeps me awake.

KENNY

When's the last time you slept, Aunt Myra?

MYRA

I don't know—before the bank heist. Three days ago?

KENNY

Aunt Myra!

MYRA

No big deal. I'll sleep after I get over the border. I'll keep saying, Canada, Canada, Canada, and it will lullaby me down to sleep. Can you hand me that Coke?

(Kenny hands Myra the Coke so she can down her pill.)

KENNY

I thought you told me not to drink Coke. That the Coca-Cola Company was a mega-conglomorate whose imperialist profits fuel the war.

MYRA

(Enjoying the Coke) Ah . . . It's true. But it's got caffeine. Sometimes you've got to use the system to crush the system.

147

KENNY

That's so true.

MYRA

What happened to the guard I hit?

KENNY

She's okay. She's gonna lose her little toe on her left foot. The one you ran over. Mom say's they're gonna nail you for attacking someone in uniform.

MYRA

I didn't see her in my rearview mirror. There she was, with her bright orange safety patrol sling, signaling traffic, and the next thing I know, she's screaming and holding her foot and hopping to the curb.

KENNY

It was an accident. You didn't mean to run over her little toe. It's gonna be okay.

MYRA

I'm really strung-out. I can't move like this. I'm going to take one toke for the road, just to take the edge off. Want some?

(Myra lights a joint; Kenny perks up expectantly as Myra starts to toke up. Myra inhales and passes the joint to him. Kenny inhales, gasps, chokes. Several puffs back and forth.)_

MYRA

Cannabis always calms me down.

(She starts to giggle. Kenny inhales, starts giggling too.)

KENNY

What's so funny?

MYRA

Our slogan for the street action during the election: "Vote on the Street; Vote with Your Feet." And that poor guard— *(They splutter with laughter. Myra suddenly has a mood swing; scared)* Oh man, Myrna's right. They're going to nail my ass. Once you've drawn blood from a pig, they really come crashing down on you. Like Chicago.

(Kenny, getting stoned, is staring and fingering the sock.)

KENNY

Aunt Myra—what's with the sock?—

MYRA

—The sock?

KENNY

Why did Mom make such a big thing out of the sock?

MYRA

I used to tease her by leaving my socks on her side of the line in our bedroom. Ages ago. Back in Mineola.

KENNY

Oh.

(Suddenly, Myra starts to sniffle.)

MYRA

Oh man, Kenny, I would do anything if I could just wake up in my bed in Mineola again and none of this had happened— Hacker, the bank job, the feds, the price on my head.— You know what happened to me this week, Kenny? It's like I woke up. I've been walking around in this trance, and all of sudden, when Hacker jumped in the car with the money and his guns, and started screaming, I woke up. I suddenly thought:

This is real, you asshole, this is happening.

KENNY

You did it for the Cause, Aunt Myra.

MYRA

Yeah, but which one? First there was the Peace Movement. That's when I first did marijuana. We put daisies in the rifle barrels of the National Guard. I thought if we all just came together, the people, the cops, the narcs, the working class, the bankers—then the war would just stop.

KENNY

That's deep.

MYRA

That's naive, Kenny.

KENNY

Oh.

MYRA

You know, if you spend enough time in the kitchen cooking for the young men who organize Peace marches, you really want to see blood and guts and gore.

KENNY

Groovy, Aunt Myra. So why'd you do it, Aunt Myra?

MYRA

Well, it's like the story of Jacob and Esau. This cat named Isaac was living in the land of the Chanaanites, which was way out in the suburbs. And he prayed to Yahweh for children to mow his lawn. And God musta heard his prayer, cause his wife Rebecca got buns in the oven. Twin buns. But these twin buns were as different at birth as Wonderbread and Croissants. **There was bad blood between them. No one could clear up the bad blood.** One son, Esau, came out all big and hairy and red-necked. The other twin came out sensitive and smooth and small. And this child, Jacob, was a loner in the land of the Chanaanites who were always grunting: "Our Country! Love it or Leave it."

And when their time came to kick the bucket, all of the Chanaanite fathers hoarded their goats and cattle and land and gave it as a blessing to one son, while the other children could go diddle themselves. And Jacob got wind of this deal coming down. He went out and skinned a sheep and padded himself with its skin, and Jacob went to Isaac's bed and said, "Bless me daddy-O." Isaac squinted and said, "You sound like that little hippy-freak Jacob." But Isaac took his large, leathery hands and felt Jacob's arms and torso and neck and said, "But you're big and hairy and red-necked. Chip off the old block. You must be Esau. You get my goats!" And Jacob got all the goats and sheep and cattle and loot, and quickly, he rode the hell out of town. **He went on a long, long trip far across the borders.** He went to the land of the peaceful farmers where they divvied up all his loot and opened up a food bank. **And he never came back.**

KENNY

What happened to Esau?

MYRA

Who knows? He moved to a nice neighborhood in Great Neck.

KENNY

In a year or so, Aunt Myra, things will cool down and you'll come back.

MYRA

With Tricky Dick in the White House? I don't think so.

KENNY

Mom says you're paranoid.

MYRA

Listen, there's a few things your mother could teach J. Edgar Hoover about sabotage. Of course I'm *paranoid*. I shared a bedroom with her for *seventeen years*.

(Beat)

Look, Kenny—it's great to be with you. But it's dangerous, honey. I've got to move out tonight. I'm being shipped out in a meat truck to Buffalo. And then I'll make it across the border with friends from there. . . . I'll bet it's gonna be a long time before I'll be able to eat hamburger.

KENNY

Aunt Myra? Before we go—can I ask you something? What happened to my mother?

MYRA

I really don't know what goes on in your mother's head, Kenny. She . . . she said she heard voices. The doctors said shock therapy would be the best thing. So I . . . so I . . . well, actually your grandmother and I . . . we went along and signed the papers.

KENNY

(Doubt) You—you signed the papers? *(Beat)* I'm sure you thought it would help.

(Just then, Myra hears a noise in the hall.)

MYRA

Shit!!—I knew it!

(Kenny creeps to the door and motions for Myra to be quiet. He cautiously opens the door a crack.)

KENNY

It's okay. It's the neighbors. It's time for us to go, Aunt Myra.

MYRA

Wait a minute—Kenny—I've been thinking—what if I don't go? What if I decided to surrender to the authorities instead?

KENNY

What?

MYRA

(Increasingly hysterical) No—see—they're really in a nasty mood right now. It will be worse if they catch me running. But if I just walk in—or if you delivered a letter to the police station for me, and I could walk in after—if I say I'm sorry to the security guard, if I say I'm sorry to the bank, if I say I'm sorry to everyone who's ever lived in Mineola—I'll bet I could get some time off the sentence. But if I run—they'll throw the book at me. Or worse—they'll shoot me in the back. I've been in this room for twenty-four hours thinking this through—and maybe I'm not thinking straight right now—but is the cause worth it? I mean, I suddenly got this feeling that five years from now, I'll wake up, and all of our slogans and chants and songs will suddenly seem like the anthems of the Campfire Girls—

KENNY

Aunt Myra—you're going to make it. I'm going to help you. I'm going with you.

MYRA

Don't be ridiculous, Kenny—

KENNY

I'm not going back to Great Neck! I fucking hate Great Neck! What is there to do in Great Neck? Argue in school about whether or not we can read Catcher in the Rye?! I missed Woodstock because my bourgeois mother wouldn't let me go! And by the time I get out of high school I'll miss the whole movement! My mother is a zombie and my father is a joke. You've got to take me with you!

(Myra covers his mouth.)

MYRA

You're gonna get us both arrested.
(They listen, tense. Then they relax, a little)
You can't come with me to Canada—all I need is to add federal and international kidnapping charges to my indictment—

KENNY

They won't find us; I'll change my name and my hair and my face and go underground with you—you were supposed to be my real mother; it was all some kind of mistake—she's not my real mother—

MYRA

Shh-shh—Kenny. Listen, in a world of Catholics, everyone's a mistake.

KENNY

You can't do this on your own. You're tired.

MYRA

I know. But—you've got to finish high school.

KENNY

There are high schools in Canada.

MYRA

Kenny! I can't. Don't. I can't think straight.

KENNY

I've got it all planned. The feds will be looking for a single woman terrorist. But—they won't look twice at a mother and her son holding hands as they cross the street.

MYRA

A mother and her son . . . Oh—God forgive me. Yes, Kenny, Yes! Right Now! Kenny! Now! Before I change my mind. We'll go down the fire escape.

KENNY

Yes!

(As they start toward the window, they hear the front door of the apartment building being hammered down) You Get Out of Here, Aunt Myra. Go, go, go! I'll try to hold them off. —Get Out of Here!

MYRA

Shit! —How the hell did they get the address? —Oh, sshittt!

(Myra flies across the room and clambers out the window. Kenny looks around for furniture to brace against the door. He sees the single chair and angles it under the knob. There is the sound of a door giving way, and then we hear footsteps running up five flights of stairs. Kenny goes to the window, looks out, hesitates. Just as he decides to climb down, the front door is burst down by the two federal agents who come into the room with drawn guns. Myrna comes behind them, dressed in a London Fog overcoat.)

MYRNA

Kenny!

(Kenny slowly faces his mother and raises his hands above his head in surrender.)

1989

The Corporate Headquarters of Concerned Americans for America. The top floor of an office tower on Madison Avenue. The stage is divided into a very glossy lounge and a sound booth where broadcasting is now in progress. An "On the Air" sign is lit in the lounge in red.

Back lit, and in shadow, we see a woman seated at the console of radio equipment, wearing headphones, and speaking into a microphone. We hear a voice-over:

VOICE-OVER

Don't Touch That Dial—right after Rush, right before Paul Harvey—we've got "Talk Back, Get Back, *Bite Back*" with M. R. O'Brien, president of Concerned Americans for America. WWKY—Talk Radio—the station you love to hate. Now for the latest hit tunes by Crystal Lewis, Twila Paris and Amy Grant.

(As she breaks from her weekly broadcast, the lights come up on the lounge where we can hear M. R. O'Brien on a speaker. Ben, age fifteen, stands in the shadows and waits nervously for the broadcast to end. The red "On the Air" sign flashes off. The sound booth door opens, and Myrna O'Brien enters. At first she does not notice Ben.)

BEN

Excuse me. Mrs. Myrna O'Brien?

(Myrna looks at Ben. She is startled, almost by a ghost. He steps into the light.)

MYRNA

(Gasping) Oh my God—

BEN

Aunt Myrna? I'm your nephew—Benjamin. Myra's son.

MYRNA

Stand in the light where I can see you. *(Ben steps into the light and raises his hands; he is holding a book)* What is that you're holding?

BEN

It's your book! *Profiles in Chastity*! I just wanted you to . . . autograph it.

MYRNA

You have no idea about the hate mail my show receives. What is it you want from me?

BEN

Just to see you in person.

MYRNA

All right. Mission accomplished?

BEN

(In a burst) I listen to your radio show every week! You're not ashamed of our legacy as Anglo-Saxons. That's what we're taught in school—to be ashamed of being white males. We get hit on the head about the holocaust and date rape, and I hate being in high school! What about all the Germans who died! What about singing Christmas carols! What about roast beef and the Lord's Prayer and standing for the national anthem at football games where there used to be skinny cheerleaders with all-American knockers—

MYRNA

—There is a God! *(Myrna laughs)* Your mother doesn't know you're here?

BEN

No. She—Sarah thinks I'm at the Museum of Natural History for school.

MYRNA

Oh yes—the quaint myth of evolution. Who's Sarah?

BEN

She's my . . . she's my mother's, uh, significant, um, spousal—

MYRNA

—Oh yes, yes, yes, you needn't go on with all the buzzwords. Benjamin has "two mommies." Well. Would you like to sit? *(Ben, nervous and excited, sits)* What grade are you in, young man?

BEN

Ninth.

(The electronic buzzing echoes under the following.)

MYRNA

Right after I lost my husband, I placed Kenny in a military school when he was in ninth grade. I think it's important for young boys to be surrounded by strong men as role models. And then after the academy, he went straight into the Citadel, and then into the service. For the rest of his life, Kenny will have a very straight spine. *(Ben sits up straighter on the sofa)* Have you thought about what you'd like to be when you grow up?

BEN

I want to be a commentator like you, Aunt Myrna! And a writer. Like you or Barbara Bush. I really liked her book.

MYRNA

Mrs. Bush wrote a lively, engaging account of White House life from a dog's perspective—a great role model for young people.
    (Beat)

So, Benjamin. I'll bet your mother has been putting you to bed for years with stories about me as a boogeyman to scare you.

BEN

She has. She also told me she used to do things to you when you were kids to bug you. Dirty socks and stuff . . .

(Myrna laughs nostalgically.)

MYRNA

Oh, yes, Myra's socks.

BEN

See, I knew you'd be like this!

MYRNA

Like this?

BEN

You know, warm and really smart—and really, uh, nice.

MYRNA

Instead of?

BEN

Well, you know, Mom thinks that conservatives go around blowing up abortion clinics and stuff—

(Myrna and Ben laugh.)

MYRNA

Your mother and her imagination. Your mother still works, I gather, for Planned Parenthood in Nassau County?

BEN

Yes. I'm afraid she does. . . . Can I—can I ask you something?

MYRNA

Certainly.

BEN

What happened to my mother?

MYRNA

Oh. Well. I'm no expert in these things, of course. You know, your mother as a young woman had quite a "social life"—so why she turned out this way, only scientists in the future will tell us. Of course, five years in prison "sharing the soap" didn't help. —But I think we choose our way—I think willpower and the right values determine our path.

BEN

So—you don't think . . . um, a way of life—

MYRNA

—Homosexuality is *not* genetic. I do worry about environment but then—see, Benjamin, if we were living in a decent, God-fearing state like Virginia, I could sue the state for your custody. But no, we happen to live in New York.

BEN

I mean, Mom and Sarah . . . do the best they can—

MYRNA

—I'm sure they do. Listen, I've had a lot of experience, traveling this great land and all over the world. And let me tell you what I see: I see, sitting beside me, a promising young man who—through willpower and thinking—can end up as a leader among men.

BEN

So you think it's a matter of choice?

MYRNA

Some things are *not* a matter of choice. Having a baby is not a choice. It's a gift from God. But who you love, how you live is a *choice*. We don't talk enough these days about willpower. And young people need to hear that. Every Saturday night, all over America, husbands and wives *will* themselves to make love to their spouses. They don't want to—but they will themselves to do it. —Do you see what I'm getting at?

BEN

(Utterly confused) I think I do. It would help if I knew who or what my father is. . . .

MYRNA

Oh yes. When I was growing up, unwed mothers were raising bastard children. Now they're raising turkey-baster kids. Well. Your mother and her . . . her "friend"—

BEN

—Sarah?

MYRNA

Yes—I imagine they've told you all about the Facts of Life.

BEN

(Blushing) I know the . . . "essentials." They mostly talk about *love* all the time. That it doesn't matter who I love when I grow up—as long as I'm *happy*.

MYRNA

Well, then, you know all about—I hate using the technical words. Like the word that Rhymes with "Worm." —See, the left uses technical words to dehumanize what they're doing. They say fetus instead of baby. "Not brought to term" instead of abortion. And they say—the word that rhymes with "worm"—

BEN

—I think I know what you mean—

MYRNA

—Right. I like to call them the Little Guys. I think of the Mystery of Creation as a crowd of Little Guys pushing their way to the front—and each one of us never knows which

Little Guy will become King of the Hill. Every Life is a lottery of luck—the luck of the Little Guy. So it doesn't really matter who your father is, Benjamin—he could be Charlie Manson or Henry Mancini. One never knows. That's why every life is sacred. We all get the Luck of the Little Guy Draw.
(Beat)
Now I hope you don't mind me asking you a question—

BEN
You can ask me anything!

MYRNA
See, I've never actually met a living woman who "lives" your mother's "life-style." I heard that a young woman on Senator D'Amato's staff was allegedly a . . . a . . . *(Myrna hears buzzing)*

BEN
A lesbian?

MYRNA
Yes. Thank you. And I very much wanted to meet her and ask her questions, but she got fired before I could. So you're the only one I know to ask.

BEN
What do you want to know?

MYRNA
Well: Which one is the man?

BEN
(A little horrified) The man? It doesn't really work like that. . . .

(Electronic buzzing.)

MYRNA
My money's on Myra. I mean, I get scared when I think about—just the thought of kissing a woman makes my stom-

ach heave—doesn't it make you feel a little seasick? Well, of course not, you're a young man, it wouldn't make *you* want to heave—you'd have to visualize kissing someone different, like— *(Myrna gets a little dreamy)* —Ohh—like a young, strapping Olympic athlete with nice, firm pecs—

BEN

Aunt Myrna!

MYRNA

Or a man on a construction crew on a hot summer day who's just removed his undershirt. —Do you think that's what they meant when they said one man's meat is another man's poison? —Still, I feel that in my line of work I should really know just what it is they "do" in bed. —Of course, it's all academic—I'm not going to go out and do any firsthand research—ha-ha! Sometimes I think there's a special room in hell for sinners just filled with women who have to "kiss" each other for eternity.

(Ben stands in a sweat.)

BEN

Um—I have to be going now, Aunt Myrna—I really appreciate your time and—

(Myrna stops him.)

MYRNA

—Do you see Kenny very often?

BEN

Yes. He comes over for dinner about once a month. Usually with Conchita and the kids.

MYRNA

And every Christmas. Is he . . . is he all right?

BEN

I think he's fine, Aunt Myrna. I'm really sorry.

MYRNA

Well, he's made his choices. I know he holds me responsible—for sending him away and for your mother's arrest. But if I hadn't taken a firm stand, he was heading for a lifetime of hairdressing or interior decorating. Of course, he would have made good money. But thanks to me, he's a happily married man. Choices!

BEN

I'm sure in time he'll appreciate it.

MYRNA

I wonder.

BEN

And I want to thank you again for letting me meet you—

MYRNA

Oh! My book! Didn't you want my autograph?

BEN

Yes! Please. Very much.

(Myrna takes a pen out of her purse.)

MYRNA

How shall I inscribe it?

BEN

(Shyly) Well, tomorrow is Sunday—and it's my birthday—so could you please write "Happy Birthday"?

(Myrna writes and hands Ben the book.)

MYRNA

Happy Birthday! How old are you?

BEN

Fifteen. Tomorrow.

MYRNA

How nice. I'll bet you and your mother and . . . and your—

BEN

—Sarah—

MYRNA

—Yes—are going out for a big Sunday dinner.

BEN

No. Mom's in Chicago. She won't be home until Monday. Some National Board Meeting that she couldn't miss. She said we'll do something next weekend.

MYRNA

A mother should be with her son on his birthday.

BEN

Even if she were home, we'd have to drag her away from the clinic.

MYRNA

On a Sunday? Isn't the clinic closed on a Sunday?

BEN

Yeah. But she works all the time.

MYRNA

Oh. So tomorrow no one's at the—that's too bad. I hope you have a happy birthday, Benjamin.

BEN

Thanks, Aunt Myrna.

(Myrna sees Benjamin to the door.)

MYRNA

I'm very proud of you. Keep the faith. In another ten years, your mother's "tribe" is going to lose the war. Very soon, if I and my friends can help it, there will come a time when your mother and "Sarah" will have to wear lipstick and heels and try to pass; when they will once again refer to each other as roommates; and where any desire to fulfill their biological destiny will be stopped by the Children's Welfare Agency who will take custody of any offspring they might have. We will never give this country back.

BEN

Thank you for all you're doing. You're nothing like my mother.

(Ben leaves. Myrna stands in thought. Overlapping music up into Dream Sequence Number Three.)

Dream Sequence Number Three

The Voice, a disc jockey with a reverb, announces on the air:

Dream Sequence Number Three.
Talk Back, Get Back, Bite Back. Myrna O'Brien Will Take
Your Calls.

(A pause. And then seductively, Myrna leans into the micro-
phone:)

MYRNA

"Kwaanzaa."
  "Feliz Navidad."
  "Kristallnacht."
What do these words have in common?
They all evoke a festive time of year. They're impossible to
spell, hard to pronounce and . . . they're *"foreign."*
But most of all, these words are printed at taxpayer
expense in new editions of high school textbooks, teaching
concepts that the school board calls *"multi-culturalism."*
All-American words have been deleted to make room for
these foreign words. Words like: Apple Pie. Norman Rock-
well. Spiro Agnew.
Our cultural values are being eradicated to make room for
illegal immigrants and militant feminists who want to rewrite
the Anglo-Saxon, Christian history of this country.
When tofu-eating-feminazi-fetus-flushing critics scorn us
for not offering positive portrayals of women, I Have To Laugh.
What about Mary Todd Lincoln? Julia Dent Grant? Ida
Saxton McKinley? Florence Kling Harding? Mamie Dowd Eisenhower? Thelma Ryan Nixon? And countless other women who
served under and on top of the great presidents of this country?

It's time to offer wholesome portraits of American Traditions, and to stop "multi-culturalism" in our schools. I will take your calls.

(*Myrna sits in front of a phone panel, with headsets and mike. She looks a bit frightened. Throughout the dream, the sound is distorted, distant and alien. There is a buzz on line one, and she answers it*) Talk Back, Get Back, Bite Back—you're on the air.

(*And then the echoing sound of Jim Tracy, sobbing:*)

JIM'S VOICE
Myrna? Myrna? Baby? There's—there's no one here—for God's sake—Myrna, can't you just talk to me a little—

(*We hear Myrna snap a button, disconnecting the caller.*)

MYRNA
Whoopsy. Looks like we've lost caller number one.

(*We hear Myrna push another button.*)

MYRNA
Get Back—you're on the air.

(*Over line two comes the excited voice of a five-year-old girl:*)

CARMELA'S VOICE
Feliz Navidad, abuela! Soy Carmela!

(*Myrna eagerly rushes to answer in bad Spanish:*)

MYRNA
Feliz Navidad, hija! Ha sido una buena chica? Esta tu padre? Is your daddy there? Carmela—Don't hang up on Grandma—No quelga—No quelga—Carmela—put your daddy on the phone—

(There is the sound of Kenny, now grown, picking up the phone:)

KENNY'S VOICE

Hello?

MYRNA

Kenny? Kenny! Don't hang up—we're on the air—for God's sake, Kenny—can't you just talk to me a little?

KENNY'S VOICE

No-no-no-no-no-no-NO.

(There is the sound of a phone hanging up, and a dial tone. Myrna tries to regain her composure.)

MYRNA

That was Ken O'Brien Junior, just saying no.

(Another phone call. Myrna stares at it, not wanting to answer, but finally she does:)

MYRNA

Bite Me—

(Myra's high school voice fills the air; the electroshock therapy noise rises as the current passes through Myrna's headset. Breathing and heart beats up.)

MYRA'S VOICE

(Urgent whisper) Myrna—when the air-raid siren comes on, don't hide under your desk. Run down the hallway and out of the building.

MYRNA AND MYRA'S VOICE

Stay away from the building.

MYRA'S VOICE

Run to the playground. I'll be waiting.

MYRNA

We can make it home before the blast. Mom says we're to climb into the shelter and lock it, if she and Daddy don't make it home.

MYRA'S VOICE

And after the blast, Mom says not to unlock the door. Not even if she and Daddy beg us too.

MYRNA

There's enough water and canned lima beans to last us six months of nuclear winter.

MYRNA AND MYRA'S VOICE

We'll take care of each other. Okay?

(Just then the air-raid siren comes on.)

MYRA'S VOICE

Myrna? Myrna? Get to the Door Now.

(The sound of nuclear holocaust echoes into Scene Six.)

SCENE SIX

A Few Days Later

Lights have come up on an empty parking lot outside Planned Parenthood, Nassau County. A Sunday afternoon. Through-out the scene, there is intermittent ticking. Myrna, dressed as Myra in a tailored suit, enters from stage left. She carries a small box, neatly wrapped in brown paper. She looks around her. In a state of excitement, she carefully tucks the box under her arm, and draws out a cellular phone from her handbag. Myrna dials.

MYRNA

Jerry? Agent Firebird here. *(Myrna stifles a giggle)*
Operation Jane Roe. Not yet. Well, yes, of course I have it. I'm a little scared of putting it down. —Do you know how many speed bumps there are in Nassau County?

I haven't had this much fun since Halloween! You should see this wig and how I'm dressed—I'll bet this is exactly how Myra dresses when she networks with NOW members and Emily's List—

—Where should I plant it, again? The right window in the back is my sister's office and the left window is the lab. —How much time is on that timer? Oh? Oh. No, I parked two blocks away—

—Wait a minute, Jerry, there's a woman walking down the street. I'll call you from the car. Over and out.

(Myrna quickly stuffs the receiver back into her purse. Sarah enters from stage right, and stops.)

SARAH

—That's the new outfit you bought in Chicago? *(Sarah bursts into laughter)*

MYRNA

I think it looks . . . rather nice.

SARAH

My God—stockings! And you've shaved! That's the kind of Power Suit I always thought your sister would wear.

MYRNA

Thank you.

SARAH

It gives you . . . quite a figure. Well—don't I get a kiss?

(Myrna is trying to figure out who this woman is, hoping it's just a friend.)

MYRNA

Of course.

(Myrna delivers a polite peck on the cheek.)

SARAH

That's what I get after a week away? I want a real kiss. Oh come on—there's no one around—come here, lover.

(Myrna's eyes bug. Sarah embraces her.)

MYRNA

I . . . I can't. I'm scared to.

SARAH

You . . . you don't want to kiss me?

MYRNA

I can't. I'm scared I'll—give-you-my-cold! I'll give you my cold.

SARAH

Are we feeling a little shy?

MYRNA

Yes I am.

SARAH

It's like we're strangers again, isn't it? And we have to get re-acquainted all over again. Slowly. Intimately. *(Sarah approaches Myrna)* Once Benjamin is in bed.

MYRNA

Yes! Benjamin. Where is he?

SARAH

He's been moping all week, thinking you were going to miss his birthday. *(Indicating the box)* Is that what you got him in Chicago? What is it?

MYRNA

It's a—surprise!
  (Before Myrna can stop her, Sarah grabs the box and rattles it to find out what it is) No, no, no sweet Jesus—*don't do that*! *(Sarah stops, stares at Myrna)* It's—it's very very fragile.

SARAH

Fine—don't tell me. Keep your little secret! —Speaking of secrets—

MYRNA

—Listen—"Sarah"—I need to make a quick call—to see if I can "cancel" something. Will you just hold that and *don't move*?

(Myrna rushes off, stage left.)

SARAH

(Calling after) Please be here when Ben arrives or you'll ruin the surprise!

(Sarah is left holding the box, waiting. Ticking up. She can feel the box stir, slightly. Her curiosity is getting the better of her. She starts to gently pry at the paper, and starts to remove some tape at one corner in order to peek beneath the wrapping. Just then, Myra rushes in—stage right—if the actor can manage it. Sarah is almost caught.)

MYRA

Hello, sweet stuff.

SARAH

That was quick! —Here, hold this. *(Sarah thrusts the box into Myra's hands)*

MYRA

What?

SARAH

Ben's birthday present.

MYRA

This is a strange way to begin my homecoming. —Do you like my new outfit?

SARAH

Very much. Listen—Myra—remember during our last session with Patsy you asked me to tell you about trouble immediately instead of handling it myself?

MYRA

Benjamin! Don't tell me, he demonstrated for White History Month.

(Sarah takes a book from her shoulder bag, holds it behind her back.)

SARAH

It's nothing that dramatic, honey. *(Sarah shows Myra the book. Myra is appalled)*

MYRA

Profiles in Chastity. Is this a joke?

(Sarah hands the book to Myra.)

SARAH

Read the inscription.

MYRA

"Happy Birthday Ben." Oh. Oh no. He hates me.

SARAH

He doesn't hate you, Myra—

MYRA

(Waving the book) —So what is this—love? This is a slap, this is a dagger, this is a bomb—

SARAH

—This is why I "handle" things myself.

MYRA

Okay. I'm calm. How do you suggest we handle this?

SARAH

Sometime later this week, why don't you try to have a heart-to-heart between mother and son?

MYRA

Don't laugh . . . but he . . . scares me.

SARAH

He scares you! He's your son, Myra.

MYRA

I know, but . . . I get scared when . . . I look into his eyes. The way he looks at me. Like he expects something. I can't live up to it. Only my sister can. Sometimes I think I've borne my sister's son.

SARAH

Oh no. He's your son. Everything's an absolute with you two—there's no gray.

MYRA

I work my fingers to the bone. Because the day will come that Ben will be left to his own devices by us because we have to work late. He'll borrow our car to study at the library. But instead he'll drive to the lover's lane off the Jericho Turnpike where, because they canceled sex education courses in Nassau County, he'll innocently knock up a girlfriend in the backseat of our car. And when that day comes, thanks to me, he and his girlfriend won't have to make the hard choices between coat hangers and marriage! We will never give this country back!

SARAH

I think we just need to spend more quality time with Ben.

(Sarah takes the book back and puts it in her handbag.)

MYRA

I hope my next decade is better than this one. Here—hold this. I left something for Ben in my office. *(Myra gives the box back to Sarah and exits)*

SARAH

—Myra! Don't make any phone calls! Don't read the mail! He'll be here any minute.

(Myrna returns, jittery, from stage left.)

MYRNA

Give me the box, please. Some things can't be "canceled."

(Myrna makes a grab for the box. Sarah refuses to let go.)

SARAH

You're not planning to work any more tonight, are you? — I've got to tell you, that Scarsdale Country Club outfit on you is making me hot. I don't know if I can control myself in public—

MYRNA

—Try. Listen, I have to—

SARAH

—Oh, and who made you the prude all of a sudden? Who brought home the leather straps from that little women's boutique last Christmas?

(Myrna turns a shade green.)

MYRNA

I'm not sure we should get into this in public—

SARAH

—Oh. Right. Be coy. And who was it that broke the straps the very first time we tried—?

MYRNA

My. That was a treat. Give Me That Box Now.

SARAH

Only if you let me get into "your box" tonight.

(Completely mystified, Myrna takes the box.)

MYRNA

Hold on to that . . . "thought." I left Ben's . . . card . . . behind
. . . the building.

*(Myrna exits left with box. Sarah glances at her watch. Ticking
up.)*

SARAH

(Calling after her) I'm here, ready and . . . waiting.

(Sarah spruces up the way lesbians do. Myra enters.)

MYRA

Sarah—Ben isn't here yet? I just got a call from Planned Parenthood in Philadelphia—they received an anonymous phone tip
this morning. A splinter group of Operation Rescue is going to
bomb one of our clinics. We have to go on alert. I'll call Chris
and ask her to come down so we can go to dinner.

SARAH

Of all days—

MYRA

(Already exiting) —I know. I'll "delegate authority." Okay?—

SARAH

Patsy's going to be so proud of you!

(Myrna reenters. Ticking up. Sarah blinks at her.)

MYRNA

Mission Accomplished.

SARAH

You are just buzzing like a little bee today—where's his gift?

MYRNA

I'm giving him something nicer.

SARAH

(Staring at Myrna's breasts) There's something . . . different about you. . . . Did you change your hair?

MYRNA

Yes. No. Let's go.

(Myrna makes a move to go but Sarah grabs her and flirtatiously straightens Myrna's blouse, collar, etc.)

SARAH

Listen, hon, we're going to a steakhouse Ben wants to go to—so please don't make any cracks about Barbara Bush. You know how he idolizes her.

MYRNA

Okay. Let's go.

SARAH

And don't bring up your sister's book. Stop calling it "*Profiles in Frigidity,*" okay? He's just using her to get to you. He'll grow up and see her for what she is.

(Myrna suddenly stops being in such a rush.)

MYRNA

Oh? Exactly what is she?

SARAH

I'm sure she's just a human being, not some monster who goes around blowing up abortion clinics. . . .

(Ticking up. Myrna takes Sarah's arm and starts guiding her offstage.)

MYRNA

Let's go meet Ben, grab a steak, and toast Mrs. Bush—

(As Myrna drags Sarah to exit:)

SARAH

Boy, this is a switch! I thought I'd have to come in and drag you away from your desk.

MYRNA

From . . . my desk?

(A horrible thought crosses Myrna's mind as she realizes Myra is in her office.)

MYRNA

Sarah—I have to tell you something.

SARAH

Oh no. You didn't—did you?

MYRNA

Didn't what?

SARAH

Did you—did you sleep with another woman in Chicago?

MYRNA

My God! No!

SARAH

Because you've been acting . . . a little strange. You left for Chicago right after our fight and—we have to give the counseling time to work. Every family is dysfunctional when there are teenagers in the house—and I'm trying to listen to my intuition—and I've had this feeling all week that you're in danger. That I'm in danger. And I know you find Patricia Ireland very charismatic. And I know she's more than happily married—but I've been having these images of you casually meeting her after the Contraceptive Technology Panel—a drink, the need to discuss the platform language—it's been tormenting me. But I would want you to tell me. Did you?

MYRNA

No! I swear to you—you are the only woman I have ever even wanted to—kiss.

(Myrna, almost hypnotically, starts to kiss Sarah. Just then Ben enters.)

BEN

Aunt Myrna? What are you doing here?

(Sarah turns, horrified, and stares at Myrna.)

MYRNA

Benjamin. I am . . . so sorry. You told me—your mother was in Chicago. Or I would never have— Please. You've got to—

BEN

—Where's Mom?

(Both Sarah and Ben look at Myrna with an awful suspicion. Ticking loud.)

MYRNA

Please both of you—stay calm.

BEN

Mom? Mom?— *(Ben runs offstage to the building)*

MYRNA

No! Ben!

Stay away from the building.

SARAH

Oh My God. You're bombing the building.

(Sarah runs after Ben. Myrna turns to leave, but is stopped by the sound of amplified breathing and the echo of Myra's childhood voice.)

MYRA'S VOICE

Myrna? Myrna?

(The sound of amplified gulping and soft heart beats. Myrna concentrates in a trance:)

MYRNA

Myra. Get to the *door* NOW.

(She is answered by the amplified sound of heart beating louder)
Myra!

(As Myrna runs toward the clinic we hear her voice reverberating in an echo of "Myra get to the door NOW." A beat later, as the lights dim, we hear the sound of a loud explosion.)

Dream Sequence Number Four

The Voice narrates:

Dream Sequence Number Four.
Myra in Mineola Dreaming of Myrna in Mineola Dream-
ing of Myra. Together Again.

*(Lights start to come up on the left side of the stage. We
see Myra in her nightgown sit upright in her bed on the oppo-
site side of the stage as The Voice whispers and prompts:)*

Myrna? Myrna? Are you asleep?

*(The lights dissolve into a dark and stormy night. Thunder,
lightning. Myra, age sixteen, is back in her bedroom in
Mineola, and has been lying in her twin bed stage right.
Myrna lies in the bed at right. A violent crash of thunder.)*

MYRA
Myrna? Myrna, are you asleep?
(The sound of amplified breathing.
*Another crash, closer. Myra, scared, gets out of her bed
and tiptoes to an imaginary line in the center of the room)*
Myrna? I'm going to cross over the line, okay? The line divid-
ing your half from mine? I know you told me not to cross it
except in case of fire or nuclear emergencies but— *(A terrific
crash. Myra leaps into bed with Myrna)* That last one was
pretty close, wasn't it?
*(No response. Thunder rumbles. The sound of The Voice
gulping)*
Myrna? Can't you just talk to me a little?

(Pause. Myra's a little closer to crying. The sound of an amplified heart beating)

Myrna? If you talk to me right now, I will never, ever leave my dirty socks on your side of the line.

(More lightning)

You're scaring me!

(The heart beats faster; Myra fights for a little control) I can hear your heart beating. I know you're not asleep, Myrna. That's okay. Just keep pretending. That you're asleep. I just want to say . . . Myrna? I'm sorry. Okay? I'm sorry . . . for everything.

(No answer, but we can feel Myrna listening. Myra summons up all of her courage, and in a whisper:) And I really wish . . . I wish we could be closer.

(An even louder crash and flash of lightning: Myrna sits up and turns to Myra, kissing her on the mouth during the lightning bolt. Suddenly, the twin beds slide together to form the double bed that Myra shares with Sarah in Mineola)

Myrna!

(Myra sits up remembering the dream. There is the sound of thunder moving off in the distance. Sarah wakes up, turns on the light.)

SARAH

Myra? Honey? You okay? . . . Were you dreaming?

MYRA

Yes. . . .

SARAH

About your sister?

MYRA

I don't remember.

SARAH

You're never too old for nightmares.

MYRA

That crazy, murdering bitch almost blew up Ben, you and me
to pieces.

SARAH

We almost blew up together, just like any other happy nuclear
family.
(*Beat*)
Let's try to get some sleep. Okay?

MYRA

Okay.
(*Beat*)
Sarah?

SARAH

Yes?

MYRA

Sometimes I miss the fifties.

SARAH

Uhm-hmm.

MYRA

In the fifties we were scared of Boris Karloff. We weren't scared
of riding the Long Island Railroad or working in clinics.

SARAH

I know. Let's not talk anymore tonight.

(*Sarah turns off the light. A beat, as the two women start to
doze. Suddenly eerie, sci-fi horror music of the fifties creeps
in. Myra sits bolt upright in the bed in terror. Sarah turns on
the light.*)

SARAH

What? What is it?

> MYRA

I feel **like I'm being watched.** Like **she can hear every word I'm saying.**

> SARAH

Your sister doesn't have that kind of power, Myra.

> MYRA

What about the clinic?

> SARAH

Coincidence. Luck.

> MYRA

I had just hung up the phone when I heard her voice: **Get To The Door Now.**

> SARAH

I believe you. Lots of people hear voices. Paul on the road to Damascus. Joan of Arc.

> MYRA

Son of Sam.

> SARAH

And now I want you to hear a voice. It's telling you: Go To Sleep. Close Your Eyes. . . . We'll talk about it in the morning.

> MYRA

(Still spooked) Okay.

(Sarah turns off the light and holds Myra. They start to drift.)

> SARAH

Think you can sleep?

> MYRA

Yes.

(A beat.)

SARAH

Sleep tight, honey.

(The light fades more; a pause, and then, in the dark room, we hear The Voice answer:)

Sweet dreams.

(Myra rises again and peers into the dark as Doris Day's "I'll See You in My Dreams" begins to play. Lights dim to black-out.)

End of Play

Paula Vogel's *How I Learned to Drive,* is the recipient of the 1997 Lortel, Drama Desk, Outer Critics Circle, New York Drama Critics and OBIE awards for best play. Her newest play, *The Mineola Twins*, is scheduled for production at The Roundabout in New York City. Her play, *The Baltimore Waltz*, won the OBIE for Best Play in 1992, and her anthology, *The Baltimore Waltz And Other Plays*, which also includes *Hot 'N' Throbbing, Desdemona, And Baby Makes Seven* and *The Oldest Profession*, was published in 1996 by Theatre Communications Group.

Ms. Vogel's other awards include the Rhode Island Pell Award in the Arts, the Robert Chesley Award in Playwriting, The Pew Charitable Trusts Senior Residency Award, a Guggenheim, an AT&T New Plays Award, the Fund for New American Plays, and several National Endowment for the Arts fellowships. She is a member of New Dramatists.

Her plays have been performed at theatres such as the Lortel, Circle Repertory, American Repertory, the Goodman, Magic Theatre, Center Stage and the Alley, as well as throughout Canada, England, Brazil, Chile and Spain.

She is currently working on the film adaptation of her play, *The Oldest Profession*, and on a new book for a revival of the musical, *On a Clear Day*. Other works in progress include screenplays, a novel, *Travels Without Charley*, and a new play.

She lives in Providence, Rhode Island.